CROSSCURRENTS / *Modern Critiques*
Harry T. Moore, *General Editor*

Poets, Critics, Mystics

A Selection of Criticisms Written Between 1919 and 1955 By John Middleton Murry

EDITED BY

Richard Rees

PREFACE BY

Harry T. Moore

SOUTHERN ILLINOIS UNIVERSITY PRESS
Carbondale and Edwardsville

FEFFER & SIMONS, INC.
London and Amsterdam

Copyright © 1970, by Southern Illinois University Press
All rights reserved
Printed in the United States of America
Designed by Andor Braun
Standard Book Number 8093–0414–7
Library of Congress Catalog Card Number 78–83668

Contents

Preface

Because there has been so much contention over John Middleton Murry, as man and critic, it is good to have this volume of his previously uncollected criticism, put together by Sir Richard Rees, who also contributes an Introduction that places Murry in perspective.

Since his death in 1957, Murry has been somewhat in eclipse, little known to the newer generation of readers. Born in a South London suburb in 1889, Murry attended Oxford, where he began his editorial career as co-founder of the advance-guard magazine Rhythm which, after he took it to London, became the Blue Review. At this time he began his relationship with Katherine Mansfield, whom he later married. His widespread influence as a critic began with his study of Dostoevsky in 1916. During the First World War, when he was medically exempt from service, Murry served in the Intelligence Department of the War Office. In 1923, the year Katherine Mansfield died, Murry founded the Adelphi, a controversial journal which was a magnet for intellectuals. During that decade he brought out various books, including an important and influential one on Keats as well as The Problem of Style, based on a series of lectures delivered at Oxford.

Those who met Middleton Murry after the late 1920's felt that they already knew the man because he seemed, physically at least, to embody the caricatures of him by D. H. Lawrence and Aldous Huxley: here were the wispy smile, the tonsure-like effect caused by a bald spot, the bemused stare into space,

the agony of the faun on the Cross. Murry's book on
Lawrence (Son of Woman) which came out in 1931, the year
after the latter's death, was a psychologically motivated examination which displeased the friends of Lawrence. Aldous
Huxley said it was "about a Lawrence whom you would never
suspect, from reading that curious essay in destructive hagi-
ology, of being an artist." In later years, Murry wrote of
Lawrence with greater detachment and made some notable
statements about him, particularly in Love, Freedom and
Society in 1957, the year of his own death.

And now we have, to add to Murry's critical volumes—
many of them still in print, at least in England—this collection of his reviews and journalistic criticism. The collection
differs somewhat from other volumes of Murry's criticism
in that most of these pieces were written for the Times Literary Supplement, under that journal's rule of anonymity. That
rule is often an unfortunate one, for it tends to encourage
nastiness, and in recent years a new British school of rudeness
has too often been represented in the pages of the TLS—too
many angry young critics who had unhappy childhoods have
used the journal to carry on their own sense of personal
outrage. This was not true in Murry's case; indeed, the
anonymous reviews forced him into a controlled type of writing different from the subjective rhetoric in which he so often
indulged in his signed pieces. The lengthy anonymous review
is a severe test for a critic, and Murry passed it notably. See
for instance his review, in the present book, of F. R. Leavis's
D. H. Lawrence: Novelist. Murry was largely in disagreement
with Leavis's findings, and plainly said so; but he keeps the
argument on the ad rem scale and never once descends to
the ad hominem level. He showed that he could disagree
without being disagreeable.

Yet Murry regarded himself as "an absolutely emotional
critic." At least that's what he told Katherine Mansfield he
was, in a letter in 1919: "If a work awakens a profound response in me, then I sit up and try to find what it is that is
working in me. In other words I am an absolutely emotional
critic. What may seem intellectual is only my method of
explaining the nature of the emotion." Well, Know Thyself,

in the Delphic phrase; but perhaps Murry was doing an injustice to his intellect. It may have been dominated by his emotions, but it was certainly there.

Murry was among other things a very learned man. In this book, for example, consider the essays on Hölderlin and Chateaubriand. They indicate something of Murry's range in world literature. In the informatively wise Introduction which follows, Sir Richard Rees reminds us that Murry "was a pioneer in introducing Proust to English readers." But he wrote mostly of British writers, including Shakespeare and his own tempermental opposite, Swift. A recent issue of the D. H. Lawrence Review (vol. 2, no 1, Spring 1969) had a number of articles assessing Murry, in which experts in various fields surveyed Murry's wide-ranging accomplishments; these scholars and critics found a certain amount of fault with Murry's work, but also discovered much in it that is valuable. In a predominantly friendly (however critical) review of Murry's book on Shakespeare, C. G. Thayer of Ohio University, a specialist in the English Renaissance, wrote two sentences about Murry which I cannot resist quoting. The first of them reflects the kind of feeling one often has after an immersion in Murry, while the second sentence projects the conclusion which one is eventually bound to reach: "Murry was no doubt a strange, eccentric, neurotic man—generous, impulsive, quixotic, mercurial, naïve, nutty, and bright—with enough problems to suit almost anyone. But although he could never achieve success as a literary artist himself, he lived with literature, thought about it, responded to it, loved it; and surely these are important qualifications for any critic we are to take seriously."

For any critic we are to take seriously: and surely we can take seriously the work of the man printed in this book. As I suggested earlier, the imposition of anonymity did not serve as a disguise for splenetic or affective attitudes, but rather induced a kind of control which manifests itself in the judgments as well as in the style and manner of these writings— the ones which are anonymous, that is. As Richard Rees points out in his Introduction, the review of Jung has a bit of flippancy and levity; but, as that editor also indicates, this occurs in a signed review. Sir Richard's Introduction, which is a significant contribution to Murry criticism, now follows. That old friend of Murry's, once his associate as an Adelphi editor, provides a most judicious Introduction to these selections.

HARRY T. MOORE

Southern Illinois University
May 1, 1969

Introduction

A considerable part of Middleton Murry's literary criticism was written for The *Times Literary Supplement*, whose reviewers are anonymous; and this may be one of the reasons less discreditable to their discernment for the comparative failure of his contemporaries to recognise Murry's value as a critic. It should be of interest today to read some of his criticisms of important books on their first appearance, especially as the authors were in some cases almost or quite unknown at the time when Murry first wrote about them.

In the early 1920's Murry was a leader of the generation of intellectuals which included Aldous Huxley, T. S. Eliot, D. H. Lawrence, Katherine Mansfield, and Virginia Woolf. He was one of the first champions of Lawrence and Eliot and was a pioneer in introducing Proust to English readers. He was married to Katherine Mansfield, and in 1919–21 Aldous Huxley was his assistant editor on the *Athenaeum*. Eliot, who was then working in a London bank, had been Murry's first choice for this job, and although he decided not to leave the bank he contributed to the *Athenaeum* many of the essays which he later collected in *The Sacred Wood*. Some of these essays were written, as Eliot mentions in the 1928 preface, directly at Murry's suggestion; and Murry's own review of Bridges on Milton (1921), the first in this volume, indicates how close the contact between his mind and Eliot's must have been at that time.

But unlike Eliot (whose opinions developed in a sense even more opposed than Murry's to the prevailing intellectual fashions), Murry soon became unpopular on account of his mysticism and his politics. He continued, however, for more than thirty years to contribute to the *Times Literary Supplement* essay-reviews of which many have never been republished over his name. The greater part of the present volume consists of a selection from these reviews. The only exceptions are the review of J. S. Phillimore, which appeared in the *Athenaeum*, the reviews of Bridges and Jung, which appeared in the *Nation and Athenaeum*, and the last five essays, which appeared in the *Aryan Path*. The editors of the last named magazine deserve gratitude for having encouraged Murry to write on subjects related to their theosophical interests, in spite of his disagreement with some conspicuous features of their doctrine.

That Murry was an outsider, and out of sympathy with the intellectual, cultural, and spiritual drift of his time is the most essential fact about him; and one could say the same of D. H. Lawrence or T. S. Eliot if one was introducing selections from their work. It is true that Murry appears in these pages more often as a literary critic than as a scolding prophet; but if any of his criticism continues to be read in the twenty-first century it will have survived for the same reason that the writings of Lawrence and Eliot will have done. All three of them possessed the spark of vitality and the realistic vision which save their possessors from the illusions of materialist-humanist progressivism. They did not condescend to the wisdom of the past or imagine that modern enlightenment has improved upon it. However much or little they may have understood about political and technological progress, and however much they might have disagreed about it among themselves, they could recognise a decadent culture when they saw one. "Remember," said D. H. Lawrence in his essay "The Education of the People," "that the souls of the working people are only rendered neurasthenic by your false culture." And if it is true, as was asserted in a well-known lecture a few years ago, that we have today not one culture but two, so much the worse; for both are equally false.

But cultural decadence is not incompatible, in the short run anyway, with technological progress, and if the almost identical government programmes in all countries of the world today are even approximately carried out, then the twenty-first century will resemble a sort of world-wide concentration camp *de luxe*. Universal higher education will turn out ever smoother models of what Eliot called the "industrialised mentality"; and the arts of self-expression and the techniques of communication will be perfected—only to reveal that there is nothing to express except the empty shibboleths of progressive humanism and nothing to communicate except displays of exhibitionistic frustration.

The spleen of Lawrence, the nostalgia of Eliot, and the nausea of Aldous Huxley's *Brave New World* are characteristic of serious twentieth-century artists; and they are confirmed from a different point of view by the labour theories of Hannah Arendt and also by a thinker who actually experienced modern labour conditions, Simone Weil. To borrow Hannah Arendt's terms from *The Human Condition*, civilised man has already become incapable of *work* and capable only of *labour*, whether intellectual or manual; and what he is labouring towards is a world in which there will not even be any need for labour—a world in which our present state of "productive slavery" will be replaced by a state of "unproductive freedom." In a world which has lost the conception of work there will be no place for science or art. The artist will be no more than a man with a "hobby"; and as for science, more than thirty years ago when Simon Weil was writing *La Condition ouvrière* she knew that it had already become impossible for any scientist to be more than a "scientific drudge."

Do these considerations seem too broad and sweeping to be relevant as an introduction to a book of literary criticism? In the case of Murry or any serious critic, in a time like the present, they cannot be left out of account; and it is for the same reason that I have decided, after some hesitation, to include here Murry's criticism of Jung's *Psychological Types*. This review has a tone of crude levity, even flippancy, which is highly uncharacteristic of Murry, (though it is characteristic of him that this review is a signed one); and, moreover, he expressed similar ideas more academically in two essays in *Discoveries* ("English Poetry in the 18th century" and "A Note on the Madness of Christopher Smart"). The longer essay, written sixteen years later, on Freud's *Moses and Monotheism*, is a better expression of Murry's mature appreciation of the thought of the two pioneers of modern psychiatry. But the very crudeness of his rejection of psycho-analysis helps to make his point clearer. Murry was a valuable critic because he was able to diagnose the cultural malady of our time and because he was one of the few who have seen clearly that it is the symptom of a spiritual malady. He understood, and in his apparently flippant review of Jung he makes the point unanswerably, that there is no cure for spiritual degeneration in art-for-art's-sake, nor in psycho-analysis, nor in any progressivist philosophy. And though we may still lack the courage to be cured, we can at least be grateful to a writer who diagnosed the disease and who exposed and discredited quack remedies.

The tone of the Jung review is all the more striking by contrast with Murry's habitual decorum and courtesy as a reviewer. For example, the serious reservations about Leavis on Lawrence and Empson on Ambiguity are expressed with exemplary moderation, and the altercation with Eliot over Shakespeare and Seneca is as amicable as it is lively. Murry himself was perhaps the most unscrupulously abused and vilified author of his day, and not least by Aldous Huxley. His generous appreciations, when he was editing Peace News in the 1940's, of Hux-

ley's pacifist writings, and also his kindly anonymous review, not included in this volume, of *Adonis and the
Alphabet* (*Times Literary Supplement,* 30.9.1956),
seem to me remarkable as coming from the victim of the
caricature which Huxley had perpetrated a generation
earlier in *Point Counter Point.*

Thanks are due to the editors of the *Times Literary
Supplement,* the *Aryan Path,* and the *New Statesman
and Nation,* for permission to reprint these essays, which
reveal Murry as one of the most distinguished critics of
his time and with a competence extending over a wider
field than almost any of them.

RICHARD REES

London
May 1969

I   Poets and Novelists

1

Milton's Prosody

Few literary inquiries are more fascinating to writers themselves than the discussion of the technical practice of the great ones before them; few seem more otiose and pedantic to the reader at large. The reader feels, and rightly feels, that the secrets of the workshop are for the workmen themselves, and that he has no more call to be interested in them than in the complicated network of ropes and laths which are the skeleton of a scene in the theatre. His concern is with the finished product: to approve or disapprove. And not only is there this negative lack of interest in the technical practice of poetry, but it is stiffened and given the substance of a positive hostility by a vague feeling that the more a poet's work lends itself to technical analysis, the more stilted and artificial it must be.

Once more there is something sound and healthy in the instinct; a residue of reason lies behind the unreasoned feeling. Technique is, after all, only an instrument, and the poet is to be judged only by the sounds he draws from it. As our fascination with the manner in which he manipulates it increases, our power of attention to the prime content of his work is weakened; we find ourselves admiring a craftsman, not an artist. And though this may be due to our own infirmity, an incapac-

Milton's Prosody, with a Chapter on Accentual Verse. Notes by Robert Bridges. Revised Final Edition. Oxford: Clarendon Press. (*Nation and Athenaeum*, 28 March 1921.)

ity in ourselves to follow the two entwined threads that compose a poet's achievement, the chances are that the poet himself has become entranced by his own technique. He has forgotten that his main object is to cross the river; he is engrossed with the attempt to walk over it on the ferry rope.

Milton is altogether too great a poet to come under this summary censure; yet, if we are to be honest, we cannot permit him wholly to escape it. We cannot help being struck by the progressive desiccation of his poetic genius, even if we take no interest in his technique. From the "Nativity," the "Allegro" and "Penseroso," "Lycidas" and "Comus" to "Paradise Lost" is a long journey, in which much spontaneity and freshness has been wasted; from "Paradise Lost" to "Samson Agonistes" is another journey, not so long, but yet marked by a perceptible sacrifice of true poetic vitality. "Samson Agonistes" is a superb museum piece; it is not that living art from which we derive an enrichment and refinement of experience. Enrichment and refinement is to be had from it, but of a peculiar and esoteric kind. It is, as Dr. Bridges most clearly shows, a triumph of technique; but though it excites the craftsman in us, it leaves the rest of our inhabitant selves unmoved.

"Samson" is the extreme point of Milton's artistic progress. There his poetic vitality is at its lowest, and his craft at its highest and most elaborate. If you have been reading Milton steadily, you will hardly have observed the increasing desiccation, because your interest in the astonishing technical dexterity will have gradually supplanted your interest in the poetic content; but there is a curious lapse in the last chorus of "Samson" which recalls one with a shock to a sense of the elasticity of the finest English poetry:

> But he, though blind of sight,
> Despised, and thought extinguished quite,
> With inward eyes illuminated,
> His fiery virtue roused
> From under ashes into sudden flame,

As an evening dragon came
Assailant on the perched roosts
And nests in order ranged
Of tame villatic fowl, but as an eagle
His cloudless thunder bolted on their heads.
So virtue given for lost,
Depressed and overthrown, as seemed,
Like that self-begotten bird
In the Arabian woods embost
That no second knows nor third,
And lay erewhile a holocaust,
From out her ashy womb now teemed,
Revives, reflourishes, then vigorous most
When most inactive deemed;
And though her body die, her fame survives
A secular bird, ages of lives.

The three lines I have marked with italics are a manifest disturbance of the stately rhythm of the semichorus; the movement of their falling rhythms recalls to the mind a poetic delicacy quite alien to the massive and artificial style of "Samson." The lines happen to be about a Phoenix. Turn to Shakespeare's marvellous "Phoenix and the Turtle":

Let the bird of loudest lay,
On the sole Arabian tree,
Herald sad and trumpet be,
To whose sound chaste wings obey.

The same falling rhythm; the same Phoenix. The conclusion is, to my mind, irresistible that Milton had fallen under the spell of a reminiscence of Shakespeare; the irruption of Shakespeare not only ruins the rhythm of Milton's last chorus, but also illuminates, like a sudden flash of lightning, the distance that separates the artificial poetry of Milton's final phase from the quintessential poetry of Shakespeare.

The question of the influence of Shakespeare on Milton is a large one, and to treat of it would demand much more knowledge than I at present possess. But this, I think, can be said. Milton's great problem as a poet was to resist the influence of Shakespeare, and by his endeavor to resist the influence of Shakespeare he forced himself to his magnificent, but on the whole unfortunate, attempt to impose upon English poetry a prosody and a diction that were really unnatural. To put it briefly, in fighting against Shakespeare he fought against the genius of the English language. He may have won his battle; but he lost his life as a poet.

I do not wish to force the evidence; but Milton's own poem on Shakespeare contains a confession which to me seems much more than rhetorical:

> For whilst to the shame of slow-endeavoring art
> Thy easy numbers flow, and that each heart
> Hath from the leaves of thy unvalued book
> Those Delphic lines with deep impression took;
> *Then thou, our fancy of itself bereaving,*
> *Dost make us marble with too much conceiving—*

There, surely, Milton acknowledges that the task of poetic originality for the poet who followed Shakespeare was too heavy. He prophesied truly of himself: he, indeed, became "marble with too much conceiving," and what is more, by the force of his genius, he turned English blank verse, the incomparable instrument of Shakespeare, into marble also.

Dr. Bridges greatly admires the blank verse of Milton: the man, and, above all, the poet, who does not admire it is to be pitied. But when Dr. Bridges represents Milton's blank verse as a refinement and improvement of Shakespeare's, it seems to me that he is profoundly mistaken. It is a refinement, but in the sense that a plank is a refinement on a tree, or a pianola an improvement upon a piano; a mechanical perfection has been purchased at the cost of the natural flexibility. Milton introduced into English blank verse a systematic syllabic prosody—precisely how systematic Dr. Bridges for the first time reveals—and in order to carry this classical framework he had to invent the grand style. That a single man should have done both these things is a subject for admiration and astonishment; but we must not forget that he also petrified the poetry which he reformed.

For English blank verse has never recovered from Milton's drastic surgery; he abruptly snapped the true tradition, so that no one, not even Keats, much less Shelley or Swinburne or Browning, has ever been able to pick up the threads again. I myself believe that Keats, with his miraculous sensitiveness to authentic English rhythms, would have succeeded in a task which he had made peculiarly his own, for he had confidently plunged into the Miltonic *cul-de-sac* in "Hyperion" and had returned discomfited. We have the precise and precious evidence of his letters:

> I have given up "Hyperion"—there were too many Miltonic inversions in it—Miltonic verse cannot be written but in an artful, or rather, artist's humor. I wish to give myself up to other sensations. English ought to be kept up. It may be interesting to you to pick out some lines from "Hyperion" and put a mark x to the false beauty proceeding from art, and one || to the true voice of feeling—(To J. H. Reynolds, Sept. 22, 1819.)

> I shall never become attached to a foreign idiom, so as to put it into my writings. The "Paradise Lost," though so fine in itself, is a corruption of our language. It should be kept as it is, unique, a curiosity, a beautiful and grand curiosity, the most remarkable production of the world; a northern dialect accommodating itself to Greek and Latin inversions and intonations. The purest English, I think— or what ought to be the purest—is Chatterton's. The language had existed long enough to be entirely uncorrupted of Chaucer's Gallicisms, and still the old words are used. Chatterton's language is entirely northern. I prefer the native music of it to Milton's, cut by feet. I have but lately stood on my guard against Milton. Life to him would be death to me. Miltonic verse cannot be written, but is the verse of art. I wish to devote myself to another verse alone.
> (To George Keats, Sept. 1819.)

I believe that the critical instinct of Keats which finds such unequivocal expression in these letters was absolutely right. Miltonic verse is "a beautiful and grand curiosity" which has hypnotized many poets besides Keats. Properly studied it may have enabled them to achieve a statuesque Parnassian beauty; but if ever a poet should arise with a deep and urgent poetic content to express he will be faced with Keats's problem; he will be compelled to break away from the Miltonic blank-verse prosody, and will have to create a new instrument for himself. Probably he will have to go back to Shakespeare. "Back to Shakespeare's blank verse" sounds at the first hearing less a counsel of perfection than a counsel of imbecility. Which Shakespeare? There are so many. It is certainly no good to hypostatize any phase of Shakespeare's prosodical development, which was unceasing; but it is possible, I believe, to awaken within oneself a sense of Shakespeare's direction, and to follow with an intuitive understanding his gradual liberation of himself from syllabic prosody and his increasing use of a stressed blank verse; above all, his ever more faithful fidelity to true speech rhythms.

In everything that Shakespeare wrote after "Twelfth Night"—to take an approximate turning-point—the "native music" of true speech rhythms is developed to the increasing discomfiture of syllabic prosody. The rhythmical period is allowed to work out freely. Take, for instance, Hamlet's soliloquy:

> To be, or not to be: that is the question:
> Whether 'tis nobler in the mind to suffer
> The slings and arrows of outrageous fortune
> Or to take arms against a sea of troubles
> And by opposing end them? To die, to sleep;
> No more; and by a sleep to say we end
> The heart-ache and the thousand natural shocks
> That flesh is heir to, 'tis a consummation
> Devoutly to be wished. To die, to sleep;
> To sleep: perchance to dream: aye, there's the rub,
> For in that sleep of death what dreams may come
> When we have shuffled off this mortal coil,
> Must give us pause. There's the respect
> That makes calamity of so long life.

That is surely a perfect piece of versification, and of an infinite subtlety. The three rhythmical periods, the first ending in the fifth line, the second at "devoutly to be wished," the third at "must give us pause," are allowed to override all strict syllabic prosody. The fifth line will not scan; the thirteenth has only four feet. Yet both are perfect; the dramatic weight of "Must give us pause" brings the period to a full conclusion, and similarly "by opposing end them" clinches the first rhythmical phrase. The rhythm begins again. These are, if you choose, licences; they are really characteristic Shakespearian triumphs. Read any part of "Paradise Lost" afterwards, and you will discover how much subtlety in the instrument has been lost; in other words, how much capacity to express the finer shades of emotion has been sacrificed. In Shakespeare the speech rhythm dominates the prosody; in Milton the prosody kills the speech rhythm. One has but to compare a fine passage of the later Shakespeare with a fine passage of "Paradise Lost" to have an inkling of what Keats meant by his at first sight cryptic phrase: "English ought to be kept up." Miltonic prosody necessarily means frozen English.

Dr. Bridges's study is invaluable: its importance reaches far beyond the aid it gives to a right understanding of Milton's verse; it should stimulate thought, and awaken consciousness in every modern English writer of poetry. This is a time when a real technical awareness may do more than anything else to carry English poetry out of the doldrums in which it is becalmed. It will help poets to face their problems, and to discover which way offers hope of most profitable advance. Even if they disagree, as deeply as I do, with Dr. Bridges's estimate of the value of Milton's prosody, they will be compelled to find reasons for the faith that is in them. Only by challenging Dr. Bridges's tacit assumption that Milton has established the norm of English blank verse will they be able to resist his contention that it is illegitimate to mingle syllabic and accentual verse. For everything depends upon what you understand by syllabic verse. If it is verse with the strict syllabic prosody of Milton, then indeed the mixture will be repellent to any sensitive ear; but if it is a verse built on a flexible syllabic prosody, freely admitting resolved feet and lengthened words, as Shakespeare's did, the antinomy does not really exist. Milton's prosody simply forbids such beautiful lines as:

> Burned on *the water*; the poop was beaten gold,

or

> We two that with so many thousand sighs
> Did buy *each other*, must poorly sell ourselves.

From the Miltonic point of view, which is Dr. Bridges's, the syllabic foot is suddenly supplanted by a stress foot. Yet our ear is enchanted by the variation. A prosodical scheme which makes the subtlest beauties of English blank verse illegitimate is more interesting than helpful. It is, to repeat the words of Keats, "unique, a curiosity, a beautiful and grand curosity," but it is "a corruption of our language." One cannot legislate for a language on the basis of one of its own corruptions, however magnificent.

2

T. S. Eliot on Shakespeare and Seneca

In a very notable introduction to the reprint of Newton's *Seneca* ('Tudor Translations: Constable: 2 vols.) Mr. T. S. Eliot suggests that the influence of Seneca upon Elizabethan tragedy in general and Shakespeare in particular has been wrongly estimated. He says:

> What I chiefly wish to consider are, first, the responsibility for . . . the Tragedy of Blood—how far Seneca is the author of the horrors which disfigure Elizabethan drama; second, his responsibility for *bombast* in Elizabethan diction; and, third, his influence upon the *thought*, or what passes for thought, in the drama of Shakespeare and his contemporaries. It is the first which I think has been overestimated, the second misconstrued, the third undervalued.

I am quite willing to be persuaded by Mr. Eliot on the first two points. His presentation of the evidence seems convincing; anyhow I know too little of the facts to offer any useful disagreement. On the third point I disagree with Mr. Eliot, but I do not know whether he seriously holds his own views.

With this third point Mr. Eliot deals but briefly in his introduction to Newton's *Seneca*; but he develops his position more fully in an address to the Shakespeare Association, *Shakespeare and the Stoicism of Seneca* (Milford). In that address, after a gently humorous ref-

New Adelphi, March-May 1928.

erence to various modern conceptions of Shakespeare—
"the fatigued Shakespeare, a retired Anglo-Indian, presented by Mr. Lytton Strachey . . . the messianic Shakespeare, bringing a new philosophy and a new system of
yoga, presented by Mr. Middleton Murry . . . the fero-
cious Shakespeare, a furious Samson, presented by Mr.
Wyndham Lewis . . ." he continues:

> I proposed a Shakespeare under the influence of the
> stoicism of Seneca. But I do not believe Shakespeare was
> under the influence of Seneca. . . . I wish merely to
> disinfect the Senecan Shakespeare before he is produced.
> My ambitions would be realized if I could prevent him, in
> so doing, from appearing at all.

It is baffling to compare with this the following passage from the introduction to Newton's *Seneca*:

> In a comparison of Shakespeare with Dante . . . it is
> assumed that Dante leant upon a philosophy which he
> accepted whole, whereas Shakespeare created his own; or
> that Shakespeare had acquired some extra- or ultra-intel-
> lectual knowledge superior to a philosophy. This occult
> kind of knowledge is sometimes called "spiritual knowl-
> edge" or "insight." Shakespeare and Dante were both
> merely poets (and Shakespeare a dramatist as well); our
> estimate of the intellectual material they absorbed does
> not affect our estimate of their poetry, either absolutely or
> relatively to each other. But it must affect our vision of
> them and the use we make of them, the fact that Dante,
> for instance, had behind him an Aquinas, and Shake-
> speare behind him a Seneca. Perhaps it was Shakespeare's
> special role in history to have effected this peculiar union
> —perhaps it is a part of his special eminence to have
> expressed an inferior philosophy in the greatest poetry. It
> is certainly one cause of the terror and awe with which he
> inspires us.

I do not think those two statements can be made consist-
ent, except by some slightly disreputable verbal fence
over the meaning of Seneca being "behind" Shakespeare.
But I take it that Mr. Eliot wishes to suggest that the
philosophy which Shakespeare expressed was an inferior

philosophy, having much in common with the stoicism of Seneca, whether or not Shakespeare actually derived it (at first or second-hand) from Seneca. Moreover, even this statement of Mr. Eliot's position is subject to certain qualifications. We have to remember that "even if Shakespeare had expressed a better philosophy, he would not have been a better poet": and perhaps fully to safeguard myself against misrepresentation of an elusive thinker, I should quote the following from the Address:

> In truth neither Shakespeare nor Dante did any real thinking—that was not their job; and the relative value of the thought current at the time, the material enforced upon each to use as the vehicle of his feeling is of no importance. It does not make Dante a greater poet, or mean that we can learn more from Dante than Shakespeare. We can certainly learn more from Aquinas than Seneca, but that is quite a different matter. When Dante says
>
> > *la sua voluntate e nostra pace*
>
> it is great poetry, and there is a great philosophy behind it. When Shakespeare says
>
> > As flies to wanton boys, are we to the gods;
> > They kill us for their sport.
>
> It is *equally* great poetry, though the philosophy behind it is not great. But the essential is, that each expresses in perfect language some permanent human impulse. Emotionally, the latter is just as strong, just as true, and just as informative—just as useful and beneficial in the sense in which poetry is useful and beneficial, as the former.

I will take the liberty of substituting for the second term of the comparison the other lines from *King Lear*:

> We must endure
> Our going hence, even as our coming hither;
> Ripeness is all.

I do this for three reasons. First, because in the introduction to Seneca Mr. Eliot specifically adduces them as showing the influence of Seneca; second, because

Gloucester's remark really has a tinge of pure fatalism which is dramatically entirely appropriate, whereas Edgar's role in the play more nearly approaches to that of a chorus. It is his words, if any, which we have some warrant for attributing to Shakespeare in person; and thirdly, because the emotional tone of the lines more precisely corresponds to Dante's line. A more useful comparison is therefore possible.

Now, according to Mr. Eliot, the lines are equally great poetry; but there is a difference: behind the line from Dante is a superior, behind the line from Shakespeare an inferior philosophy. But this difference is absolutely irrelevant to the quality of the lines as poetry—to their poetical strength and poetical truth. That derives from the fact that each expresses some permanent human impulse.

The question to decide is why Mr. Eliot should declare that the philosophy behind the line of Dante is great, while the philosophy behind the line of Shakespeare is not.

Now obviously so vague a use of the word "behind" invites confusions. Elsewhere Mr. Eliot says definitely that "Shakespeare expresses an inferior philosophy." Thus he uses the phrases "to express a philosophy" and "to have a philosophy behind one" interchangeably, and thereby obscures the question. For the philosophy which may be said to be "behind" Dante's poetry and the philosophy which is expressed in the line *La sua voluntate* . . . are two quite different things. We may say that behind all Dante's lines is the systematic philosophy of Aquinas, in the sense that Dante accepted his philosophy for true (which it was not) and made use of it. But *La sua voluntate* . . . does not express the systematic philosophy of Aquinas at all, any more than it expresses the systematic philosophy of Aristotle. It simple expresses the Christian attitude or belief. The systematic philosophy of Aquinas is not behind that at all, any more than it is behind "Thy will be done" in the Lord's Prayer. Philosophy, in the sense of systematic philosophy, is quite beside the question.

The only "philosophy" pertinent to it is philosophy in the familiar sense of an attitude to life. The question is simply this: Is the view of life expressed in the line of Shakespeare inferior to that expressed in the line of Dante? I do not think so. In immediate spiritual quality there is not much to choose between them—a resolution of inward conflict and an act of the soul is, to my sense, implied in both. But in my opinion the philosophy of the Shakespeare line is superior because it is purified of all theological illusion. The decision lies simply between Christianity and Reason.

But to suggest, as Mr. Eliot does, that Seneca stands in the same relation to Shakespeare as Aquinas does to Dante seems to me fantastical; to suggest further that Shakespeare derived the attitude to life expressed in "We must endure . . ." from Seneca seems to me a violation of all psychological probability. Moreover, there is no evidence for it. The quotation from Seneca which Mr. Eliot indicates as the source of the lines of Shakespeare contains nothing whatever to correspond with "Ripeness is all." I am not surprised that Mr. Eliot, while he makes the suggestions seriously in one place, in another disclaims all desire to have them seriously taken: for they land him in a position which he himself regards dubiously.

> Perhaps it is a part of Shakespeare's special eminence to have expressed an inferior philosophy in the greatest poetry. It is certainly one cause of the terror and awe with which he inspires us.

Let me repeat, Shakespeare does not express any systematic philosophy at all; and no one before Mr. Eliot has ever suggested that he did. The view of life which he expresses is certainly not inferior to that which Dante expresses. The first sentence is surely nonsense. What meaning it has derives solely from the peculiar process which Shakespeare is compelled to undergo in Mr. Eliot's mind. He isolates certain lines that appear to him to have a philosophical content; he perverts this content; he then declares that the philosophy is stoicism; then that the stoicism comes from Seneca. Each of these steps is illegitimate; each takes him farther from the reality of Shakespeare. And so inevitably Shakespeare becomes the monstrous hybrid—the greatest of poets, the least of thinkers. This monster, born of his own abuses, inspires him with awe and terror. I am not surprised.

3

Villon

François Villon has always been an idol of romantics, and Mr. D. B. Wyndham Lewis (to be distinguished from Mr. Wyndham Lewis without initials) has written a very attractive and very well-nourished romantic book about the rascal poet, who is of all French poets the one whom Englishmen take most naturally to their hearts. The most curious thing about Mr. Lewis's book is that he is apparently persuaded that, whereas his English predecessors in enthusiasm for Villon have been romantic, he is not. This is a strange and unaccountable delusion. Nothing could well be more remote from Villon's own manner than the style in which Mr. Lewis writes about him. What is romantic in Villon is totally unlike the romanticism with which Mr. Lewis regards him; and the classic in Villon, which is, of course, all of a piece with the romantic in him, meets with a certain admiration but no echo at all in Mr. Lewis's attitude towards him.

It is possible to distinguish two different impulses in the romantic attitude toward Villon of which Mr. Lewis affords us the latest, and perhaps the most complete, example. There is, first, the genuine response to the romantic "note" in Villon's poetry, which answers to Pater's definition of the romantic as strangeness in beauty. In this specific sense no more romantic poem

François Villon. By D. B. Wyndham Lewis. Peter Davies. (*Times Literary Supplement,* 12 April 1928.)

was ever written than the "Ballade des Dames du Temps Jadis." But "romantic" has another and really quite different meaning: it no longer denotes a strangeness in beauty as the predominant quality of an aesthetic object, but the attitude of mind which accords a supreme value to the quality of strangeness in beauty. There is all the difference in the world between recognizing and appreciating such a quality and making it supreme. Romanticism is therefore used to denote the disposition from which this excessive valuation of the specific romantic quality seems invariably to spring—namely, a disinclination or a positive refusal to accept conditions that are familiar and quotidian. With such a romanticism Mr. Lewis's book is pervaded. Somewhat monotonously he gives voice to a belief that in the Middle Ages all was for the best in the best of all possible worlds. What, in the given context, it amounts to is that Villon really enjoyed a thoroughly delectable life and possessed a thoroughly admirable character, the first because he lived in an age of Faith, the second because he believed in the Faith. It seems a pity that Villon was not more conscious of his blessings.

This element of what we can only call romantic Catholic propaganda mars what would otherwise be a completely enjoyable book. Not only do we weary of the author's recurrent jibes at the present day, but we are made more conscious than we should be without this reminder that his critical judgment is of an adolescent sort. It is not so much Villon's poetry in itself that he delights in as the opportunity it affords him for indulging his own fantasy. That is rich and ample; only a churlish mind could fail to extract much pleasure from it; but the embroidery is strikingly different in quality from the curt, prompt, steely words of Villon which cannot be subdued to Mr. Lewis's pattern, nor his pattern to them. The discrepancy is piquant to an extreme.

In other words, Mr. Lewis has written a good sentimental romance (to the well-known sentimental tune of "No sentimentality here") round Villon. Villon becomes "a common criminal, firm in faith and affection" —a panegyric which, we suspect, would have surprised him. To correspond with this intention Villon's Ballad "feiste à la requeste de sa mère, pour prier Nostre Dame" is hoisted into the first place among his poems, in despite of the fact that it is poetically quite inferior to a half-dozen others. But it happens to express, in no very convincing manner, the faith of a Catholic, and to be the evidence that he once did something for his mother. Possibly he did other things besides for her, though he is most likely to have broken her heart; possibly he really was affectionate; but these vestiges of virtue cannot possibly lift the poem to the level of the Ballades of the Hanged Men, or of the Past Ladies, or of "The Lament of the Belle Heaulmière." Again, though it would be rash to express an opinion upon whether Villon's religious faith was, or was not real, it seems to be perfectly clear from his writing that it was not firm. The imagination which, like Mr. Lewis's, sees Villon constantly maintained by a reserve of religion is working free of the obvious facts of his poetry. If his religion had indeed been so important to him, it is really inexplicable that it should have been so resolutely excluded from his writing. So far as the convincing expression of religious emotion is concerned, we are at perfect liberty on the evidence to hold that Villon was about as religious as a modern Apache. There is some great poetry that is saturated with Catholicism, and but for its Catholicism could not be what it is; but Villon's poetry does not belong to this kind at all. It might have been written, without losing an atom of its compulsiveness or its beauty, by a complete atheist.

Mr. Lewis himself, rather inconsistently, admits as much when he claims for Villon that he is the first "modern" European poet. By that doubtful adjective he simply means that Villon expresses certain primary human emotions which are recurrent and universal. In this sense, however, Sappho and Catullus, to say nothing of Chaucer, are just as "modern" and European as Vil-

lon. To the comprehension of a Sophocles, a Virgil, a
Dante, a Shakespeare, we have to bring something other
than primary emotion. No doubt the distinction is just
as clear to Mr. Lewis as it is to other people; but he has
failed to keep it present to his mind. If he had done so,
he would not have succumbed to the temptation to
represent Villon as a sort of fine flower of medieval
Catholicism. After all, though he was a rare poet, he was
no credit to the Faith; and had he been born in the
Suburra of the first, instead of in Paris (if he was born
there), of the fifteenth century, he would have been
much the same kind of man, and written much the same
kind of poetry.

4

Hölderlin

We can rejoice that we have now a very good English
book on one of the most fascinating and most unhappy
of German poets, Friedrich Hölderlin. Since his virtual
rediscovery by Stefan George and his circle, Hölderlin
has been the thcmc of some of the best critical intellects
of modern Germany: Dilthey, Gundolf, and Heidegger
in particular, besides Hellingrath, his modern editor. Mr.
Peacock seems to have profited by them all in the prepa-
ration of his book.

Hölderlin's life-story does not need telling. Of him it
can be fairly said that his life was in his poetry. Born in
1770, he was at twenty the friend and coeval of Hegel
and Schelling. Schiller was his hero, and Hölderlin went
to Jena to live near him. He went as tutor to Frankfurt,
to the house of the banker Gontard, whose wife, Susette
(Diotima), became his Egeria. The relation had to be
broken in 1798. In the next four years his characteristic
work was done. In June, 1802, Diotima died, and at
about the same time Hölderlin had a complete mental
breakdown, from which he never really recovered. From
1805 till his death in 1843 he was insane.

Mr. Peacock says—and our recollection confirms his
statement—that the zenith of Hölderlin's fame in Germany was reached soon after the last War. Diotima's
letters to him were published in 1921, and Hellingrath's

Hölderlin. By Ronald Peacock. Methuen. (*Times Literary Supplement*, 31 December 1938.)

great edition soon after. The moral beauty of Diotima helped to emphasize the purity of the poet's aspiration. If he was a defeated hero of the spirit there was no doubt that he was a hero; if he had demanded of life more than life could give he had demanded it not for himself but for mankind. It was a noble heart which cracked. Alike in his frustration and his fulfillment Hölderlin seems to have made an intimate appeal to all that was heroic in post-War Germany before it relapsed, under the relentless pressure of the victors, into a cynicism of despair. To be smitten by the gods, like Hölderlin, is one thing; to be crushed by demagogic brutality is another. The temper to which Hölderlin appealed could not endure, and, although his idealization of *das Volk* may have contributed to the inspiration of the nobler elements of National Socialism, he has an uncertain place in the contemporary German pantheon. He is, of course, accepted as a major German poet by those who are interested in these things, but he does not seem to have been twisted into a prophet of race or blood or soil.

Yet a prophet he is; and perhaps more positively than any other German poet he conceived of himself as the *vates sacer*. But in this he was completely without egotism. It was of the function of poetry, not of himself as the poet, that he thought highly. That function was sacred, for the poet was the priest of the divine. Mr. Peacock—we think rightly—compares him with Blake both for his isolation among his contemporaries and for the purity of his utterance, which seems to carry with it so little base or neutral matter. He can be compared with Blake also for his sense of inspiration; but whereas the divine for Blake was gradually concentrated in a power which he identified with the god of Christianity, Hölderlin sought for it in the gods. These gods of his—of whose imaginative reality his poetry convinces us—appear to have been created by a singular combination of German philosophical pantheism and a profound insight into the religious sources of Greek poetry. Hence the difference in kind between Hölderlin's enthusiasm for the Greek and that of Winckelmann or Goethe. For them the Greek genius is the pattern for all time of a perfection of aesthetic culture; for him it is rather a complete utterance in a total civilization of the divine powers of Nature, and of the right human relation to them. Mr. Peacock demurs to the frequent description of Hölderlin's Hellenism as "aesthetic pantheism," though the adjective has not in German the suggestion of triviality that it has acquired in English; but we think objection to the phrase lies less because it is unapt than because no abstract formula can do other than distort the uniqueness of Hölderlin. The fact remains that Hölderlin's creed was a kind of pantheism—though it has many varieties—and that his supreme value was beauty—though beauty is variously understood and experienced. Beauty for Hölderlin was not a thing in itself, but rather the grace attendant on a harmonious manifestation of the powers of Nature. Athenian civilization was the type of the beautiful, because Nature achieved in it her own perfect form.

It is difficult to formulate Hölderlin's beliefs in this cardinal matter of Greece without reducing them to flatness and commonplace. The reader of "Der Archipelagus" knows that they were neither commonplace nor flat. It would be hard to find in all German literature a more remarkable example of vision in the hieratic and prophetic sense than that poem. One can hardly suggest a parallel to its strange immediacy. Perhaps the nearest would be one of the earlier prophetic books of Blake—"The Book of Thel" might serve. But there is one irreducible difference between them: Hölderlin is permeated by a sense of history, and even among his German contemporaries, in whom the new historical sense was common, he possessed it eminently. Blake, who had no concern with, and no need of this—so deep was his sense that Time was only "the mercy of Eternity"—makes therefore an entirely different impression. The difference is significant. It serves to remind us that Hölderlin was definitely part of the great German idealistic movement of philosophy, religion and history, whereas the English romantic movement, to which Blake may be said to have belonged, had no such comprehensive critical background. It was a poetical movement, with philosophical implications. But in Hölderlin's finest work, unlike that of English romantics, we are always conscious that the imagination is that of the historian and scholar, as well as the poet.

> Kehren die Kraniche wieder zu dir ? und suchen
> zu deinen
> Ufern wieder die Schiffe den Lauf ? umathmen
> erwünschte
> Lüfte dir die beruhigte Fluth ? und sonnet der
> Delphin
> Aus der Tiefe gelockt, am neuen Lichte den
> Rücken?
> Blüht Ionien, ist es die Zeit? denn immer im
> Frühling
> Wenn den Lebenden sich das Herz erneut und die
> erste
> Liebe den Menschen erwacht und goldner Zeiten
> Erinnrung,
> Komm' ich zu dir und grüss' in deiner Stille dich,
> Alter.

That opening theme of "Der Archipelagus" is perhaps hardly typical of Hölderlin; but it is a strain which is never far away.

One might fairly compare it with the Greek vision of Wordsworth (in "The Excursion") or that of Keats—"the milk-white heifer lows." The difference, which is sensible, seems to be that for Wordsworth and Keats the vision is primarily contemplative; whereas for Hölderlin Greece is something that is imminent again. To Hölderlin's Greece we might indeed transfer the words of Wordsworth concerning his own experience of a revolutionary France:

> Bliss was it in that dawn to be alive
> But to be young was very heaven,

for it is indeed as though Hölderlin's participation in the
great awakening of Germany took the form of an imaginative reliving, on behalf of his countrymen, of the glory
of Athens. This was, or might be, their destiny. And,
however odd, or—at the present moment—even pathetic,
that dream may appear, we have Hölderlin's own poetry
for evidence that it was not a mere dream. When we
read in cold detachment and at second hand of his
identification of Greece and Germany it strikes us as an
aberration, just as it would if an English poet were
seriously to identify London (instead of Edinburgh)
with Athens; but when we read such a poem as "Germanien," his claim of affinity seems to be in no way
strained or uncouth:

> Wenn unsere Städte nun
> Hell und offen und wach, reineren
> Feuers voll
> Und die Berge des deutschen
> Landes Berge der Musen sind
> Wie die herrlichen einst, Pindos und
> Helikon
> Und Parnassos.

The cause of this persuasiveness is no doubt the dignity and simplicity of the poetry; but, deeper than that,
it is due to the naturalness of the combination in the
imaginative experience of one who, like Hölderlin, was
conscious in himself of the awakening of the genius of a
great nation. Germany, said Marx, is *par excellence* the
country of revolutions in theory; and even he did not
mean it wholly as a gibe. The unfolding of the German
spirit in which Hölderlin shared was a happening of
universal scope manifested in a particular nation, as such
happenings must be. Hölderlin felt it in its universality,
and so he naturally blended it with what he looked upon
as the perfect expression of nature in man—man conceived as himself the flower of nature, and godlike when
he acknowledges his dependence upon Nature's powers.
The last few lines of "Germanien" show how little

Hölderlin's aspirations for his country had in common
with contemporary Nationalism.

> Doch in Mitte der Zeit
> Lebt ruhig mit geweihter
> Jungfraülicher Erde der Äther
> Und gerne, zur Erinnerung, sind
> Die unbedürftigen sie
> Gastfreundlich bei den unbedürftigen
> Bei deinen Feiertagen,
> Germania, wo du Priesterin bist
> Und wehrlos Rath giebst rings
> Den Königen und den Völkern.

"He sees all things," says Mr. Peacock very justly, "in a
cosmic or historical perspective; love of country, in him,
is love of a new order." The eternal symbol of the new
order is Greece.

In Greece, too, he found the clue to the mission of the
poet, who reveals to the people the nature of their gods.
The poet is the instrument whereby his countrymen
become conscious of the powers on whom they depend,
and of whom they are the children. These powers the
poet experiences more directly than they; he knows, in
himself, the urgency of the divine creativeness of nature,
and is most responsive to its workings in the general
world. "Wer das Tiefste gedacht, liebt das Lebendigste."
This religious love of Life he communicates to the people, who thereby become themselves responsive to the
divine power manifest in the livingness of life. Thus the
nation becomes a spontaneous vehicle of it. One might
find the elements of this faith in Goethe; but their
combination in Hölderlin has a quality of its own which
is hard to define. Mr. Peacock, we think, succeeds admirably in conveying it in his book, wherein he courageously breaks away from the current German practice
of treating Hölderlin's development in periods, and insists rather on the interpenetration of his themes and the
continuity of his attitude. Of this attitude perhaps the
most distinctive quality is humility; and to that is due
the quality of his poetic faith. No one has ever claimed a

nobler or more glorious function for the poet than he, yet none has claimed it with a more attractive modesty. The contrast, in this respect, with Milton is noteworthy.

Some have ascribed this humility of Hölderlin's to an inheritance of German piety received in his Württemberg home. However that may be, it is genuinely religious; and possibly his upbringing and his theological education gave this particular colour to his own creed. But it is more likely that there was a natural affinity between his temper and that of Spinoza, by whose philosophy, whether or not at first hand, he was deeply influenced. He seems to have received this in the historical form which Goethe gave to it, but the ethical impress of the doctrine appears to come directly from the source. Hölderlin not merely accepts the oneness of man with nature as a doctrine, but makes it the basis of his attitude towards himself, which is entirely unassuming. He looks upon himself impersonally; and (as Mr. Peacock finely notes) even when he is giving direct utterance to his own suffering the style is lapidary.

> Wo bist du ? wenig lebt' ich. Doch athmet kalt
> Mein Abend schon. Und stille, den Schatten
>   gleich
>   Bin ich schon hier; und schon gesanglos
>   Schlummert das schaudernde Herz im
>   Busen.

It recalls, by its detachment, an epitaph from the Greek anthology; and the impression is very powerful.

Here Hölderlin is become "the voice in the night." His faith in the new order, his experience of the divine, no longer sustains him. The change in tone is no doubt to be associated with the painful ending of his relation with Diotima. But, as Mr. Peacock says, "the elegiac note (of the later Diotima poems—"Menons Klagen" in particular) does not spring only, or primarily, from personal grief at separation from a loved woman, but from the absence of the kind of life she symbolizes." The distinction is just, for Diotima is pre-eminently the sym-

bol of the harmony of love and ethical passion which
was in Hölderlin's eyes the supreme achievement of
Greece. But she was this as a living person, an incarnate
justification of his faith. And it may well be that their
separation brought him sharp up against the conflict
between the actual semi-Christian world and the new
order in the coming of which he believed. He was finding that "the wise want love, and those who love want
wisdom"; and the struggle and the suffering which he
endured are a reminder that Hölderlin's Greece was not
really a pagan Greece at all. Historical though his attitude towards it was, it was the attitude of a soul sensi-
tized by Christianity, and instinctively rejecting all gross-
ness from its conception of creative nature.

Like many others, he clung to the purification
achieved by Christianity without realizing that it was
Christian. Diotima is much rather a Beatrice guiding
him to a *vita nuova* than the priestess of Plato's "Sym-
posium." "Mein Schönheitssinn ist nun vor Störung
sicher," he wrote eloquently to Neuffer shortly after his
meeting with her. "Er orientirt sich ewig an diesem
Madonnen-Kopfe." "Madonna head" tells its tale. It is
claimed for him, though not by Mr. Peacock, that he
achieved a new synthesis between Greece and Galilee. It
is more probable that the conflict was never resolved, as
parts of "Brot und Wein" suggest. But it is no less than
justice to a great and pure poet to say that Hölderlin's
genius was of a kind to feel the need of that reconciliation and to be capable of achieving it, if it can be
achieved. Instead, he became one of God's innocents.

5

Keats

"The textual criticism of Keats would be easy—perhaps indeed non-existent," says Mr. Garrod, "if it began and ended with the printed texts. Its embarrassments proceed from the astonishing wealth of manuscript material." But it might be argued that, as a general rule, it ought to begin and end with the printed text simply because the greater part of Keats's poems were published in his lifetime, and under his supervision. Occasionally, it is true, he gave Taylor or Woodhouse a fairly free hand in correction; but few poets of Keats's age have had a friend at once so indefatigable and so scrupulous as Woodhouse. We have good reason to regard the printed text of Keats's first three volumes as authoritative—manifestly superior in authority to any manuscript, except in the rare cases of a palpable misprint, or a known editorial correction of which Keats did not approve.

In the case of the posthumously printed poems the situation is different. Here the authority of the manuscripts is superior. But it is hard to make a general rule. We should not, for instance, care to challenge, on the ground of principle alone, Mr. Garrod's reading "To know the change and feel it" in "A Drear-nighted December," although the manuscripts are unanimous in giving us "The feel of not to feel it." The poem was not

The Poetical Works of John Keats. Edited by H. W. Garrod. Oxford: Clarendon Press; London: Milford. (*Times Literary Supplement*, 24 June 1939.)

printed until 1829; and it is as certain as anything can be in this order that, whether or not the printed line is preferable to the manuscript line, Keats had nothing to do with it. Mr. Garrod says the printed line is "better poetry and better logic." If that were really so, we could reconcile ourselves to it, although it says something different from what Keats said—something less characteristic of Keats. "The feel of not to feel it" is a specific and unique sensation, which has little in common with "to know the change and feel it."

Therefore, Mr. Garrod's reading is to be challenged because it substitutes a pretty and feeble line for a forcible and ugly one. Very possibly in a hundred years' time the objection to "feel" as a substantive will have entirely disappeared. It will be accepted as a valuable alternative to "feeling," not a vulgar synonym for it. Indeed, already in established usage "feel" denotes a much more physical sensation than "feeling." The fact that Leigh Hunt used it is no argument against it: "the feel of June" is a perfectly good phrase. Browning's "the feel of the fang" shows the strength of the word. And it was apropos this very line that Woodhouse noted that Keats was fond of the substantive "feel" and would "ingraft it *in aeternum* on the language." Keats knew his own business: the word belongs to the province of "sensation" in which he was a master. The perpetuation of the unauthorized reading is to be deplored—the more since Sir Sidney Colvin and Miss Lowell fought on behalf of the original line. It is difficult to understand what Mr. Garrod means by saying the printed line is better logic, it seems to us to ruin the logic of the verse.

> To know the change and feel it,
> When there is none to heal it,
> Nor numbed sense to steel it,
>   Was never said in rhyme—

is perilously near nonsense. To heal a change may pass, though it is lax; but to steel one is incomprehensible. Again, "to know the change and feel it" has been said in rhyme over and over again; but "the feel of not to feel it" does indeed defy expression.

In the opposite direction, Mr. Garrod disregards Woodhouse's note on lines 187–210 of "The Fall of Hyperion," which were accordingly omitted from the original printed version of 1856. Admittedly, the note occurs only in a transcript presumed to be made by Woodhouse's clerk. Mr. Garrod prefers Woodhouse's own transcript (which came to light in 1904) on grounds which do not appear to us very solid; for it seems more likely that "enwouned" (for "enwombed") and "Meremosyne" (for "Mnemosyne") are due to the clerk's attempt to copy Keats's autograph than to an attempt to copy Woodhouse's more legible and more familiar writing, as Mr. Garrod supposes. At any rate there appears to be nothing to choose in the matter of authority between the two transcripts; and the note is assuredly Woodhouse's. Since it is one of the few occasions when a real problem of textual criticism arises out of Keats's poetry, and since it constitutes by far the most considerable departure from the hitherto received text, we are surprised that Mr. Garrod does not explicitly discuss it.

But this consideration of detail rapidly becomes disproportionate, and in a review may easily produce the impression that we are ungrateful to Mr. Garrod for his labours. The contrary is the case; but it needs to be made clear that this edition of Keats's poetry is less a critical addition in the classical sense of the word—as the elaborate apparatus might suggest—than a valuable aid to the study of Keats's methods of composition; as it were, a monumental supplementary volume to Mr. Ridley's "Keats's Craftsmanship." It does not, and is not intended to, replace Mr. de Selincourt's annotated edition, of which the arrangement has become somewhat confused in course of time. But occasionally, and rather capriciously, Mr. Garrod allows himself annotation. For example, he has a note on the word "Naumachia" in the poem on Nebuchadnezzar, to say that he was bothered

to guess where Keats got the word until Mr. M. Buxton
Forman informed him that there was a Naumachia at
Sadler's Wells in 1804. (This explanation is also given in
Miss Dorothy Hewlett's "Adonais.") But this note ap-
pears to be solitary in its kind, and it is difficult to
understand why Mr. Garrod admitted it.

An introductory essay on the composition of "Poems,
1817," contains a convincing defence of the correctness
of the date of what has hitherto been taken to be Keats's
earliest surviving letter—that to Charles Cowden Clarke
of "Wednesday, Oct. 9th"—which means that the letter
was written in 1816 and not in 1815 as has been hitherto
supposed, even by Mr. Maurice Buxton Forman. Mr.
Garrod's case for dating the letter in 1816 seems inex-
pugnable. If it is correct, it shows how swiftly the renewed acquaintance with Charles Cowden Clarke ri-
pened into intimacy: "My dear Sir" of October 9
becomes "My daintie Davie" on October 31. Quick work
for three weeks, yet nothing improbable in a life lived at
the tempo of Keats's. The interest of this dating is
mainly biographical, in that it enables us to place the
date of Keats's meeting with Leigh Hunt with some
certainty between October 9 and October 31, 1816. As
Mr. Garrod shows, this means that Keats's decision to
publish a volume of poetry, the collection of the material, the composition of new and better poems, and the
actual publication of the book, followed in a remarkably
brief space of time. The first review of the book appeared
on March 9, 1817. If, as now seems to be established, the
decision to publish a volume was made only at the end
of October, 1816, it is another example of the speed of
Keats's life.

The actual additions to the corpus of Keats's poetry
are, as was to be expected, slight. The preface claims to
publish two "previously unknown sonnets"; but one of
them—the more interesting of the two—had already
been published, with a facsimile of the transcript, in Mr.
C. L. Finney's "The Evolution of Keats's Poetry." Since
it is unfamiliar, it is worth reproducing:

The House of Mourning written by Mr. Scott,—
   A sermon at the Magdalen,—a tear
   Dropt on a greasy novel—want of cheer
After a walk uphill to a friend's cot,—
Tea with a maiden lady—a curs'd lot
   Of worthy poems with the author near,—
   A patron Lord—a drunkenness from beer,—
Haydon's great picture,—a cold coffee-pot
At midnight when the Muse is ripe for labour,—
   The voice of Mr. Coleridge,—a French bonnet
Before you in the pit,—a pipe and tabour,—
A damn'd inseparable flute and neighbour—
   All these are vile—but viler Wordsworth's sonnet
On Dover:—Dover!—Who *could* write upon it?

John Scott was the editor of *The Champion*, and
subsequently of *The London Magazine* before it was
acquired by Taylor and Hessey; and his "House of
Mourning" was published, Mr. Garrod says, in 1817.
These then were the verses on which Wordsworth prom-
ised to pass judgment in 1816 with the encouraging
words: "I am truly glad to hear that you are determined
to try your strength in this way as I am convinced that
you have the eye, the heart, and the voice of a Poet." He
was more discreet in his next letter, in which he suggested that Scott, being a "master of prose" might find
the achievement of a like mastery of poetry too great a
tax upon his strength. Since Scott was killed (a week
before Keats died) in the famous duel which arose out of
the attacks on Hunt and Keats in *Blackwood*, it is ironical that Keats should have disliked not only his poetry
but apparently the man himself. Brown's last letter to
Keats tries to convert him to a better mind on the
subject. Moreover Mrs. (Caroline) Scott, who had attractive black eyes, was a warm and discriminating de-
fender of Keats's first volume; and there is some probability that Scott was the author of the well-known letter
to the *Morning Chronicle*, in October, 1818, protesting
against the criticism of Keats in *The Quarterly*.
   Although, as Mr. Garrod says, the date of the preface
to Scott's book (January 24, 1817) gives us a *terminus*

post quem for the sonnet, it is hardly helpful: for not only is the style of the sonnet later than 1817, but the matter also. "Haydon's great picture" was certainly not vile to Keats in that year. And Mr. Finney is probably near the truth when he assigns the sonnet to June, 1819, on the ground, first, that that date accords with the dislike of Coleridge's voice, which made a deep and disagreeable impression on Keats in April, 1819:

> I walked with him at his alderman-after-dinner pace for near two miles . . . I heard his voice as he came towards me—I heard it as he moved away—I had heard it all the interval—if it may be called so.

It accords also with Keats's changed attitude to Haydon, which Mr. Finney plausibly supposes to have supervened on Haydon's cavalier treatment of Keats's request that he would try to repay his loan. "I shall perhaps be still acquainted with him, but for friendship that is at an end," he wrote to George Keats in September, 1819. Moreover, the sonnet is certainly reminiscent of Keats's letter-writing at its maturest. The cold coffee-pot at midnight gives a vivid glimpse of Keats in the act of composition. One would naturally suppose "the walk uphill to a friend's cot" was the walk from Well Walk or Wentworth Place to Leigh Hunt's cottage in The Vale of Health, though Hunt was no longer there in 1819. The drunkenness "from beer" as distinct from a tipsiness from wine is characteristic. And the sonnet as a whole adds more to our knowledge of Keats than could reasonably have been expected in the space of fourteen lines.

The other new sonnet, which was first printed in these pages, is an earlier and less interesting production; and, were it not for some lines in the sestet, might be anybody's; but we seem to detect the touch of the authentic Keats humour, in the juxtaposition:

> Who from a pot of stout e'er blew the froth
> Into the bosom of the wandering wind.

Not so much can be said for the two additional lines of "The Cap and Bells," nor for the "new and better version" of Nebuchadnezzar's Dream: it is hard to see wherein the improvement consists.

Mr. Garrod appears to feel that his method of including all the variations of the manuscripts from the printed text needs defence. His own defence is entirely satisfying: "It may perhaps suffice that we are mortal men, having within us immortal curiosities; curiosities not satisfied with less than the full apparatus of variants." At some time or other every student of Keats is bound to be curious to learn all that can be learned of the ways by which the poet advanced to his final perfections; and in this edition the information will always await him, conveniently gathered together. In providing the student with an indispensable instrument Mr. Garrod has done a valuable work. His expressions of critical opinion are perhaps a little inclined to condescension. Thus he comments on Keats's spelling "folorn," which occurs fourteen times in the manuscripts as against once for "forlorn":

> Even "folorn" is interesting; and when Keats interates it—
>   "Folorn! the very word is like a bell"
> —it might be thought to assume importance—indeed, an almost dangerous importance. Did Keats so sound the word? And if he did, is not the verse thinner in tone?

Once raised, the question needs to be further pursued. The spelling "folorn" does not really give any indication of how Keats sounded the word, beyond that he did not roll the *r*, and did not pronounce it as a spondee. If he had done so he might more appropriately have written, "The very word is like a knell." Instead he wrote "bell." As "bell" is to "knell" in significance, so in sound is "folorn" (as Keats sounded it) to "forlorn" as Mr. Garrod perhaps imagines he ought to have sounded it. But such a line as

> A meek and folorn flower, with naught of pride

shows plainly that Keats's way of writing the word does not mean that he clipped the first syllable of it.

Mr. Garrod also finds it "hateful to think" that Keats

sounded the words "exhalt" and "exhaltation" as he spells them: surely it is nothing worse than interesting. Keats seems to have got the word mixed up with "exhort," which brings the spelling into some relation with "folorn." "Vauted" for "vaulted" appears to belong to the same tribe of idiosyncratic spellings. Neither does Mr. Garrod like the notion that Keats pronounced "horizon" to rhyme with "Morrison" (why not with "orison"?). It is probable that he did, for he twice writes "horison" in his letters; but what is more curious is that when he corrected it to the conventional pronunciation, as he did in "I Stood Tiptoe," by changing the third line of

> There was wide wand'ring for the greediest eye,
> To peer about upon variety;
> Far round the crystal horizon to skim,
> And trace the dwindled edgings of its brim

to "Far round the horizon's crystal air to skim" he rather spoiled than improved his line. But we understand Mr. Garrod's feeling that his close acquaintance with the peculiarities of Keats's orthography has enabled him to know Keats better. Owing to his and Mr. M. Buxton Forman's labours we can now share the feeling.

6

Chateaubriand

No one, not even M. Maurois, has yet succeeded in making Chateaubriand one half so sympathetic a figure as he made of himself in "Mémoires d'Outretombe." That is his masterpiece, and it is a real one. It is the one complete expression of his genius, which was egoistic and funerary. "J'ai toujours supposé que j'écrivais assis dans mon cercueil"—a queer imagination for one whose public rôle was that of a restorer of the Christian faith. "J'ai la manie de béer aux choses passées," he also said, and it was true. "Manie" was a favourite word of his; and his ordinary way of referring to the very harmless, instinctive will to existence, which human beings share with ponies and turnips, was to call it "la manie d'être." Probably that was, more or less, how he experienced it. Life was something you attained only in a fever of exaltation, whether of ecstasy or defiance. The rest was existence, of the kind described in the "Vie de Rancé." "Restent ces jours, dits heureux, qui coulent ignorés dans l'obscurité des soins domestiques, et qui ne laissent à l'homme l'envie ni de perdre ni de recommencer la vie."

The "Mémoires d'Outretombe," therefore, is a self-portrait taken from the angle and in the light which Chateaubriand liked best of all. M. Maurois considers it as the true consummation of his career. "A vain attempt

Chateaubriand. By André Maurois. Translated by Vera Fraser. Cape. (*Times Literary Supplement,* 26 November 1938.)

to make of his life a work of art" was followed "by another—this time successful—to make a work of art on his life." This is no mere epigram; Chateaubriand, one might almost say, could only experience himself when he was dead. Death and romanticism are traditionally associated; but the nature of the association is very various. "I have been half in love with easeful death," said Keats, at a moment when he found the burden of life intolerable; and the poem in which he said it is something more than a thing of beauty. Even though we knew nothing about his life, we should have no doubt that at the moment that poem was conceived Keats felt, in every fibre of his being, that it would be "rich to die," and that life was too grievous to be borne. But when Chateaubriand tells us that he has "always singularly loved death" —and he tells us this in a thousand different ways—our reaction is entirely different; indeed, the intention is different, however nearly it may sound the same. Chateaubriand liked things best when they were dead. There is no reason to believe that he particularly liked the idea of dying. On the contrary, the impression he often makes is that of one who would find beatitude in being the sole survivor—of everything.

This curious attitude of Chateaubriand towards death has been recognized by his most penetrating critics as belonging to the essential man. Sainte-Beuve, subtlest of all investigators in this province, finds in the cries of René the key to all Chateaubriand's passionate life. In "René" we have the enigmatic intoxication with death and destruction, as it were, stark naked. "Il sort de ce cœur," he says to Celuta, "des flammes qui manquent d'aliment, qui dévoreraient la création sans etre rassasiés, qui te dévoreraient toi-même." Or it is Atala crying to Chactas:

> Tantôt j'aurai voulu être avec toi la seule créature vivante sur la terre; tantôt, sentant une Divinité qui m'arrêtait dans mes horribles transports, j'aurais désiré que cette Divinité se fût anéanti, pourvu que, serrée dans tes bras, j'eusse roulé d'abîme en abîme avec les débris de Dieu et du monde.

That is the very tempest and whirlwind of what is called romantic passion; it is macrocosmic in scale, and to a modern mind rather preposterous; but, however extravagantly, it expressed an attitude which (Sainte-Beuve thought) was permanent in Chateaubriand, and deeply influenced not only his writing but his behaviour as a lover and his conduct as a man of affairs. Sainte-Beuve's withering essay upon him in this latter capacity is classical; and it is notable that M. Maurois, although he remarks, truly enough, that Sainte-Beuve was inclined to revenge himself, in his subsequent judgment of the "Mémoires d'Outretombe," for the part he had been induced to play in the conspiracy of laudation arranged by Mme. Récamier, nevertheless endorses the great critic's judgment of Chateaubriand's political conduct. It was not the conduct of a statesman at all but of one whose romantic sympathy with lost causes, so long as they were lost, led him to glorify royalism while it was in exile but to be its most intractable servant when it was in power.

M. Charles Maurras has driven this judgment home in some brilliant sentences:

> Cet artiste mit aux concerts de ses flûtes funèbres une condition secrète, mais invariable: il exigeait que sa plainte fut soutenue, sa tristesse nourrie de solides calamités, de malheurs consommés et définitifs, et de chutes sans espoir de relèvement. Sa sympathie, son éloquence se détournaient des infortunes incomplètes. Il fallait que son sujet fût frappé au cœur. Mais qu'une des victimes, roulées, cousues, chantées par lui dans le "linceul de pourpre" fît quelque mouvement, ce n'était plus de jeu; ressuscitant, elles le désobligeaient pour toujours. Quand donc la monarchie française eut le mauvais goût de renaître, elle fut bien reçue! Après les premiers compliments, faits en haine de Bonaparte et qu'un bon gentilhomme ne refusait pas à son prince, Chateaubriand punit, du mieux qu'il le put faire, ce démenti impertinent que la Restauration infligeait à ses *Requiem.*

That is, we think, as just as it is brilliant; and nothing in M. Maurois's book suggests that he would challenge it. He does not believe that Chateaubriand's resignation from Napoleon's service after the execution of the Duc d'Enghien proceeded from devotion to Royalism or to Christianity. "It would be more true to say," says M. Maurois, "that it was the resignation itself that turned Chateaubriand into a militant monarchist." That is subtle; and so is the suggestion with which it is supported, that Chateaubriand was "a great artist, striving to make the pattern of his life a work of art" and that he "had struck, in his new found loyalty to a family, an attitude which satisfied at once his craving for aesthetic unity and his feudal honour." But M. Maurois is even more cruel than Sainte-Beuve himself when he suggests that the gesture offered him a splendid exit not merely from an official career of which he was, in fact, tired, but also an escape from the necessity of settling himself in the Valais "with none for company but a woman with a long nose and pock-marked face"—to wit, Mme. de Chateaubriand.

"From 1802 onwards"—that is, virtually from the beginning of Chateaubriand's public career—"there was a great gulf set between the real and the imaginary Chateaubriand, between the personage and the person." The year 1802 saw the publication of "le Génie du Christianisme"; and M. Maurois cannot take Chateaubriand's Christianity seriously. He had no real understanding either of the mysteries, or of the sense of sin, or of Christian humility; and "all his life he went from mistress to mistress and never showed the least sign of repentance." That is true: "Le Génie du Christianisme" had its origins in a momentary and merely emotional conversion and is, to use M. Maurras's phrase, only a requiem on Christianity. The attitude is really that of the apostrophe on the beginnings of La Trappe in the "Vie de Rancé," which concludes:

> Mœurs d'autrefois, vous ne renaîtrez pas: et si vous renaissiez, retrouveriez-vous le charme dont vous a parées votre poussière?

M. Julien Benda, whose attitude to Chateaubriand is very different from that of Sainte-Beuve, or M. Maurras, or M. Maurois, singles out this apostrophe for particular admiration, because the attitude combines a deep sense of the poetry of the past and a clear-sighted recognition of that in which its charm consists—"exclusivement à leur poussière." But that is merely to see as a virtue what Sainte-Beuve and M. Maurras regard as a vice. And a vice surely it is; it is not, as M. Benda claims, the virtue of not being the dupe of romantic illusion, but the vice of an egocentric historical imagination, which does not seek to apprehend the past as living at all. "Chateaubriand n'a jamais cherché," says M. Maurras, "dans le mort et dans le passé, le transmissible, le fécond, le traditionnel." That demanded a humility which he did not possess. His attitude towards the past of Christianity is aesthetic and spectacular; he seeks in it an occasion for emotion, not a means to self-knowledge.

We may allow, therefore, that there was no intolerable contradiction between his peculiar apologetic for Christianity and his own unedifying personal life; and it would be ungenerous to emphasize it, had he not claimed to be the chief architect of a religious restoration. In fact, the revival of Christianity owed very little to him; it was the inevitable aftermath of the experiences of a nation in revolution. But Chateaubriand had cast himself for the *beau rôle*; and since he was a verbal magician, he was a valuable instrument of Napoleon's policy of religious reconciliation. The discrepancy, as so frequently in Chateaubriand's career, was not so much between his actual professions and his conduct, as between the public estimate he demanded for himself and his real motivation. For his initial self-delusion, in 1802, he had a good deal of excuse. His book seemed to be part and parcel of the act of reconciliation between France and the ancestral religion; a review of it by his friend Fontanes appeared in the *Moniteur* following a proclamation by the Emperor on the very day of the solemn *Te Deum* in Notre Dame, Easter Sunday, 1802.

Chateaubriand undoubtedly experienced the greatest stir that ever surrounded the birth of a work of the mind. It might have been supposed that the bells were ringing, the troops were lining the streets, the bishops were officiating only to do honour to the new-born fame of the poet-restorer of religion. It was "un coup de théâtre et d'autel," a day of triumph that Chateaubriand was never to forget and that worked a change in his idea of himself. From that time forwards he conceived an almost boundless political ambition and regarded himself as one of the leading figures of Christendom. He had found himself linked with the vast designs of Bonaparte—thenceforth he thought in terms of "he and I"; and as Europe had once joined Pope and Emperor in a common awe and reverence, he desired that men should speak of "the Poet and the Consul."

From that moment, M. Maurois thinks, a split between the person and the personage began. There are two things to be observed: first, that this triumphal entry into literature, religion and politics was, virtually, Chateaubriand's début as a man of letters. The previous "Essai sur les Révolutions," published hugger-mugger in London, can scarcely be reckoned. It is hardly to be wondered at if his head was turned. The second was that Chateaubriand's position, launched on a career superior to that of the man of letters, was extraordinarily difficult. He wanted the best of two incompatible worlds, to serve God and Mammon; it is a mistake, but not many men of letters have had the opportunity of succumbing to the temptation on the grand scale. One of the consequences has been that Chateaubriand, being judged mainly by men of letters who have not had the chance of falling from such heights, has been rather hardly judged. Yet the difficulties in the way of judging him fairly are tremendous. The reality of Chateaubriand seems to disappear in the rift between person and personage. Thus, when, as Ambassador in London, he was pulling all the feminine strings at his command to represent France at the Congress of Verona, he wrote to Mme. Récamier: "This Congress has the immense advantage of bringing me back to Paris, and all this talk of politics has no other meaning than that I am dying to see you." Did he, at the moment of writing, believe it? He could not have said, himself. He was in a condition in which real sincerity was impossible. As M. Maurois puts it, "seriousness, which is a complete identity of thought and expression, was never again within his reach"—and that condition obtained from 1802 to the writing of the "Mémoires." This judgment is in essential accord with that of Joubert, in his letter to Molé:

> An undercurrent of world-weariness, which seems to spring from the vast abyss between himself and his thought, for ever drives him in search of distractions which no activity and no companionship can give him as he would have them and which no wealth will suffice to cultivate unless, sooner or later, he learns wisdom and discretion.

That is, as one would expect, a truly penetrating judgment. The great *ennui,* which was indeed no pose in Chateaubriand, was the outcome of the great insincerity; the great gulf between himself and his expression, in one who was a master of expression. It was, we may allow, the *ennui* of a great genius; and we need not be surprised that it had an immense fascination for women. A faithful account of Chateaubriand's life is largely occupied with his relations with them. It is difficult to be deeply interested. One needs to know more, or to know less. One is sorry for Pauline de Beaumont; one admires Juliette de Récamier. And we have Sainte-Beuve's word for it that one of his many mistresses said: "Oh! que cette race de René est aimable; c'est la plus aimable de la terre!"No doubt it was so; but it does not make him or them interesting to read about in this relation. And one is often visited by the suspicion that they were completely captivated by the kind of thing which Chateaubriand could not refrain from, even in his "Vie de Rancé":

> Que fais-je dans le monde? Il n'est pas bon d'y demeurer lorsque les cheveux ne descendent plus assez bas pour essuyer les larmes qui tombent des yeux.

Since the living person had dropped down the rift in the personality, Chateaubriand discovered and created himself as a unity only in retrospection. Strict introspection was intolerable to him. "Emphasis and rhetoric wrapped their studied folds about a thought which could no longer endure the naked truth. A mind disquieted and divided against itself seeks to flee the searchlight of meditation," says M. Maurois. Thus it was that, in order to experience himself as living, he had to imagine himself as dead. This, however far fetched it may sound, does seem to be the explanation of the powerful enchantment of the "Mémoires," which proceeds from something deeper than the magic of the sensuous phrase. And M. Maurois's deeply interesting book (which has been well translated by Miss Vera Fraser) has helped us to solve a problem.

7

Peacock

A volume of six hundred closely printed pages, in French, on Thomas Love Peacock is a posthumous honour to which the subject of it can hardly be conceived as aspiring, even though he might have entertained it imaginatively as one of the possibilities in the future of a world which he believed to be, indubitably, rather queer. Yet if he had read, as he certainly would have done, M. Mayoux's very substantial work, he would, we think, have been relieved and gratified to know that, at the risk of inspiring a big book, he had earned the reward of inspiring a good one. His enigmatic personality, he would have observed with a certain just complacency, lost nothing of its mystery or its charm from being regarded for a long time through a magnifying-glass. His works might be slight, his elements simple; but they were the works and the elements of a living being who was an artist. They had life in them. And life, even under the microscope, is still life: simple and mysterious.

That Peacock's life was predominantly intellectual— so much so that M. Mayoux can regard him as the type of the intellectual—gives at the outset a deceptive simplicity to any investigation of him. It seems almost self-evident that a man who spent so much of his life in expressing intellectual opinions with clarity must have

Un Epicurien Anglais: Thomas Love Peacock. Par Jean-Jacques Mayoux. Paris: Nizet et Bastard. (Times Literary Supplement, 31 August 1933.)

had clear opinions of his own. The temptation, in examining such a man, is almost irresistible to jump in with labels. For example, Peacock was a Tory satirist. Professor Saintsbury was anxious to impress that view. But Saintsbury was a peculiar sort of Tory himself. And Peacock was a very peculiar one. He is a dangerous man for one who runs to read. He must be read sitting, and degusted curiously. A single sip from "The Misfortunes of Elphin" will prove perplexing and unique.

> This pennillion-singing long survived among the Welsh peasantry . . . and may still be heard among them on the few occasions on which rack-renting, tax-collecting, common-enclosing, methodist-preaching, and similar developments of light of the age have left them either the means or the inclination of making merry.

The objection to tax-collecting was not peculiar to the Tory; and he was certainly not conspicuous in his resistance to the common-enclosing and the rack-renting, which he did himself, but not more assiduously than his brother the Whig. The man who speaks there is incapable of political classification. In that he has a romantic nostalgia for the time when these plagues were not, he might be said to anticipate the new Tories of the 1840's —the "Young England" of Lord John Manners. But since they did not propose to restore the common-land which their fathers and grand-fathers had enclosed, Peacock would have thought them a set of humbugs. Probably the nearest we could get to a similar set of antipathies in Peacock's contemporaries would be in Cobbett.

Yet to call Peacock a Radical on the strength of that would be extravagant. Although he mocked at the theory of "virtual representation" and the arguments of the *Quarterly Review*, it is, as M. Mayoux points out, his intelligence rather than his sentiments that is outraged. He would have had no objection at all to a reasoned preference for an oligarchical over a representative government; but the vicious nonsense served out by way of argument by the *Quarterly* caused him a kind of nausea.

What he really likes is intellectual honesty; and it seems to him so rare a thing that he can make some of his finest comedy—as in the case of Mr. Sarcastic in "Melincourt"—by confronting the average respectable Englishman of his day with his own motives. "I reduce," says Mr. Sarcastic, "practice to theory; it is a habit, I believe, peculiar to myself, and a source of inexhaustible amusement." Peacock certainly got a great deal of amusement out of it, and he communicates it to us. But a differently tempered man would have found it more difficult. In an idealist amusement would have blazed into indignation. Peacock is hardly ever indignant; perhaps therefore hardly ever a satirist in the full sense of the word. One feels that he has no overpowering desire for a different world than the one he lives in, except in the one regard that he would really like men to be honest with themselves.

Mr. Priestley, in his critical study of Peacock, to which at moments M. Mayoux is under visible obligation, emphasizes the element of the "baffled idealist" in his subject. The pertinence of the description depends rather on what we understand by the phrase. Most idealists are baffled. It is their nature to be. The idealist who is not baffled is rather suspect as an idealist. But the idealist who is baffled by the nature of things is deeply different from the idealist who is baffled by his own nature. And Peacock strikes us very distinctly as a man who made up his mind, in good time, that he was not cut out for an idealist, and resigned any pretensions in that kind. The very distinction and contrast between practice and theory, which is the rock on which his comedy is builded from the beginning, when Squire Headlong interrupts Escot in discourse of "theological and geological philosophy" with "Push about the bottle!" to the scene in "Crotchet Castle," when the bequest for the regeneration of the world is unanimously devoted to convivial and argumentative dinners, is, if closely considered, the negation of idealism. So far from believing, with Keats, that "the Heart should be the Mind's Bible," Peacock's point of view is that the zest of life consists in the discrepancy between instinct and idea, between conscious belief and unconscious motive. At bottom the human being seeks pleasure—Peacock argues the Epicurean position lucidly enough in his famous review of Moore—and, though there are some men to whom a better ordering of society would give pleasure, he certainly did not believe in the wisdom, and perhaps not in the existence, of men who would sacrifice their immediate comfort for their ideals. Such men would be fanatics, or heroes: and there is no room for either in Peacock's world. He is no friend to "enthusiasm." The Methodist preacher is a nuisance, with the rack-renter.

M. Mayoux's subtly told story is a story of degeneration. The Radical slides into the Conservative: the Hellenist into the classical trivialist: the devotee of Aeschylus into the addict of *compère* Mathieu and Paul de Kock. What was precariously ripe in "The Misfortunes of Elphin" becomes over-ripe in "Crotchet Castle."

> Pour tout dire d'un mot, ce que Peacock prend pour sa désillusion parfaite, n'est-ce pas dans une certaine mesure sa démoralisation inconsciente? Folliott, cynisme et sentimentalisme, épicurisme assez vulgaire en dépit du grec, et qui s'empanache de préoccupations sociales comme pour faire pièce à Mac Quedy; et Chainmail, et surtout Susannah, vue avec tant de bienveillance rousseauiste et mièvre —l'equilibre, le rare et précaire équilibre du cœur et de la tête qui était encore dans *Elphin* s'est rompu et se trouve remplacé par un douteux partage: à un Peacock tout positif, la réalité, telle quelle ou un peu pire; à un Peacock de plus en plus sentimental avec l'âge, un idéalisme facile bien à l'abri des épreuves.

On the whole that verdict is not unjust. But the process of change is subtle; and we think that M. Mayoux is inclined to make it rather too definite. Peacock's entry into the India House was, no doubt, a turning point in his career; and probably M. Mayoux is right in finding significance in the almost simultaneous composition of "The Four Ages of Poetry." But it seems rash to conclude, as M. Mayoux does, that that essay is an expression of Peacock's convictions. Whatever Peacock was, he was not naïve. Whatever we may think of the letter containing his offer of marriage to Jane Griffith at the same time, it is emphatically not naïve. But it would have been very naïve—and therefore out of character—if Peacock, at the moment he stepped into his snug place at the India House, had issued a serious manifesto to the effect that the time for poets was over, and the time for men of affairs begun.

M. Mayoux is, we think, on firmer ground when he attributes a definite acceleration of Peacock's growing conservatism to his revulsion from the violence and arson of "Captain Swing" in 1830. He very aptly quotes Charles Lamb's letter to George Dyer, in December of that year, to show the reaction of a nature at least as intelligent as, and probably more generous than, Peacock's, to that outbreak.

> It was never good times in England since the poor began to speculate on their condition. . . . It is not always revenge that stimulates these kindlings. There is a love of exerting mischief. Think of a disrespected clod that was trod into earth, that was nothing, on a sudden by damned arts refined into an exterminating angel.

Not a word of sympathy, nor any attempt at understanding the motives of the oppressed and disinherited village labourer. That the poor should speculate on their condition is the fatality. Peacock's attitude is subtler. He blames the political economists and the iron law of wages. For this particular purpose ideas and systems, to which he allows in general no influence on human actions, have the status of effective causes. Yet at the same time he exploits the outbreak as a derisive criticism of "progress," of that "grand march of intellect" which Peacock judged a facetious name for "the march of mechanics," but in which Keats, in spite of all dejection, courageously affirmed his faith. M. Mayoux wryly concludes:

Ces quelques mois d'agitation, tombant à un âge ou la méfiance chez certains hommes devient dominante, avaient fait leur effet; et après avoir brandi contre Burke la triste expression *swinish multitude*, voici que Peacock se met à parler de *rabble-rout*.

The contradiction beneath is evident. It is a moral ambivalence. It uses the degradation of the people, which is the outcome of economic conditions, to justify the refusal to attempt to change those conditions; and it is the psychologically inevitable outcome of a radicalism that was never more than intellectual. The radicalism of Peacock, like that of so many others of his time, and others more pretentious than he, was really a dilettantism. When confronted with the necessity of personal sacrifice it wilted away; and in Peacock's case, as in the case of the others, by a sort of instinctive legerdemain, an insidious substitution was made between the conception of a spiritual aristocracy and an aristocracy of economic privilege. M. Mayoux well expresses one aspect of this evolution.

Peacock, comme la plupart des intellectuels sincères, comme l'épicurien Stendhal, mais comme Flaubert aussi, comme Taine, comme Renan, est devenu un aristocrate. L'intellectuel une fois fixé, peut-il sans se trahir nier une hiérarchie des valeurs, des plaisirs, ou la mettre au second plan? Qu'importent ses valeurs, ses plaisirs, ses goûts, au plus grand nombre? Les sacrifier, quel anéantissement de soi, de ce qu'on estime le plus en soi, et dans le monde tel qu'il nous a été légué. Est-ce courage ou lâcheté? Est-ce générosité ou faiblesse? . . . La majorité est fait de sots ou de demi-sots. L'intellectuel est presque fatalement conduit, contraint par l'hostilité ou indifférence sournoise de la majorité, à confronter comme elle, deux minorités: une minorité coopté, secrète, dont il est, une minorité qui habite plus souvent les mansardes que les palais; et puis la minorité des classes dites supérieures, des classes qui ont eu des générations d'oisifs pour raffiner leurs plaisirs, pour cultiver la grâce, pour rechercher ou prétendre rechercher la beauté.

That illuminating comment conveys the real purpose of
M. Mayoux's excellent book. It does indeed exhibit and
explore Peacock as the type of the intellectual confronted with the problems of modern society. For the
world in which Peacock lived, and from which he finally
withdrew into Epicurean isolation, was essentially our
own world. Peacock's distinction, among his contemporaries, was that he carried an intellectual awareness of his
own position further than they. He shared Stendhal's
horreur d'être dupe, and could not confuse himself with
the transcendental tergiversations of Wordsworth and
Coleridge. Hence he is modern in a sense in which they
are not.

For good reasons, the editors have had to exclude from
this, the first volume of the two that will contain Peacock's poetry in the Halliford edition,* all poems which
he did not himself publish. Therefore his earliest work,
"The Monks of St. Mark," has no place in it. Not only is
the volume a little duller than it might have been for
this necessary exclusion, but the reader is given, if he
considers this volume alone, a slightly false impression of
Peacock's evolution. There is only the clever Shakespearian cento which served as preface to "Palmyra and
Other Poems" (1806) to put him on his guard. An
astute reviewer, no doubt, would have been roused by
the contrast between that witty piece of verbal acrobatics
and the solemn frigidity of the verses which followed;
and he would have concluded that the author was not
what he appeared or was trying to appear. But the clue is
slight, and easily missed. Had "The Monks of St. Mark"
stood at the head of the poetry, it would have been
clearer that Peacock, at this time at least, was forcing
himself to expression in a kind for which he was not
fitted. "Palmyra" (in the first version, 1806) is depress-

* The Halliford Edition of the *Works of Thomas Love Peacock.*
Edited by H. F. B. Brett-Smith and C. E. Jones. Volume VI. *Poems.*
Constable.

ing enough; it has few virtues, and the assumed dignity of the manner is wofully contradicted by the hotch-potch of the rhythmical design. Nevertheless, one can imagine Peacock at twenty-one deceiving himself about it. It is far harder to make real to ourselves the state of his mind when he persuaded himself that the "Farewell to Matilda" was not a joke:

> Matilda, farewell! Fate has doomed us to part,
> But the prospect occasions no pang to my heart;
> No longer is love with my reason at strife.
> Though once thou wert dearer, far dearer than life. . . .
> Repent not, Matilda, return not to me:
> Unavailing thy grief, thy repentance will be:
> In vain will thy vows or thy smiles be resum'd
> For love, once extinguished, is never relum'd.

To conceive Peacock, however, young, writing that without his tongue in cheek, is difficult. But since the shorter poems in "Palmyra" are nearly all of the same order, we have to believe that he did take himself and them quite seriously. He had made up his mind to be a poet. Certainly his first volume gave no evidence that he was capable of achieving any literary distinction at all. He appears curiously insensitive to rhythmical beauty or verbal felicity. He was even rash enough to employ the word "relume," which Shakespeare had lifted to the empyrean of poetry. He uses it again in the pseudo-Norse "Fiolfar":

> The kiss of her love broke the spell of the tomb
> And bade life and rapture her beauty relume.

And six years later in "The Philosophy of Melancholy" (1812) he makes a still more precise attempt to master it:

> But when shall spring's Promethean torch relume
> Man's sovereign strength, or beauty's roseate
>   bloom?

It is less unsuccessful than the previous attempts; but that is all.

In the same year came his revised version of "Palmyra." That the poem had been immensely improved, there is no doubt. Only one-eighth of the lines in the former version were perpetuated, the rhythmical commonplace was largely eliminated; and it is not impossible to understand why Shelley, now at the age of Peacock when he produced the first "Palmyra," should have thought the concluding lines the finest poetry written in his time:

> But ne'er shall earthly time throw down
>   The immortal pile that virtue rears;
> Her golden throne, and starry crown
>   Decay not with revolving years;
> For He, whose solemn voice controlled
>   Necessity's mysterious sway,
> And yon vast orbs from chaos rolled
>   Along the elliptic paths of day,
> Has fixed her empire, vast and high,
> Where primogenial harmony
> Unites in ever-cloudless skies
> Affection's death-divided ties;
> Where wisdom with unwearying gaze
> The universal scheme surveys,
> And truth, in central light enshrined,
> Leads to its source sublime the indissoluble mind.

That certainly marks the highest point reached by Peacock in his published poetry before "Rhododaphne," which does not come within the scope of this volume. It is better than anything to be found in "The Genius of the Thames," together with which it was published. That is an altogether disappointing effusion, for Peacock really knew the Thames; but in his cold-blooded panorama any reach of the river seems like any other. Peacock never did possess the true pictorial gift; and his poem is like one of the contemporary "topographical and descriptive" volumes put into mediocre verse and deprived of the illustrations for which we now chiefly value them. It achieves a mild autobiographical interest at the moment when Peacock, travelling down-stream, reaches Oxford.

Inevitably, he takes the opportunity to apostrophize Science, who

> beneath those classic spires,
> Illumes her watch-lamp's orient fires,
> And pours its everlasting rays
> On archives of primeval days.

But the advised reader, remembering that Peacock was a good scholar and that he had not been at either university, is alert for a reservation. It is duly made, as we might expect, at the cost of a digression:

> Yet lovest thou, maid, alone to rove
> In cloister dim, or polished grove,
> Where academic domes are seen
> Emerging grey through foliage green?
> Oh, hast thou not thy hermit seat
>   Embosomed deep in mountains vast
> Where some fair valley's still retreat
>   Repels the north's impetuous blast?

In other words, in the Welsh mountains, where Peacock in these days chiefly lived.

The most interesting of the serious poems in this book is "The Philosophy of Melancholy." It is, as a poem, scarcely better than "The Genius of the Thames," and inferior to the revised "Palmyra." But it shares with the former the mild autobiographical interest, for it contains (as Mr. Priestley has pointed out) a vague "romantic" portrait of Jane Griffith as

> that fair form, ah! now too far remote
> Whose glossy locks on ocean-breezes float;
> That tender voice whose rapture-breathing thrill
> Unheard so long, in fancy vibrates still.—

and it shares with the conclusion of "Palmyra" the adumbration of a thought. For the most part it is tedious verse-spinning. Peacock seems to have determined to write a "philosophic" poem in four parts, although he had no philosophy to put in it. His method of filling his pages is to make melancholy responsible for a good many

things no one would think of associating with it. But at
the end of his fourth part he asks a question which, in
spite of the language, may have had some genuine urgency for him:

> And shall the savage faith, by phrensy taught,
> Nerve the wild spirit with all-conquering thought,
> While polished man, by sacred science led,
> Shrinks in the blast, and bends his weary head?

"No," he replies to the question that has now become
more familiar. We must make

> The mind, that wisdom wakes, that feeling fires,
> Soar on the wings of that ethereal flame
> By nature kindled in its infant frame,
> To elemental light's all-circling sphere
> Triumphant o'er the ills that wound it here.

And he ends with a translation of a fragment of an
Orphic hymn. This conclusion is obviously akin to that
of "Palmyra." But there is no evidence in the poetry
itself that Peacock held his faith seriously; and there is a
tell-tale note to the effect that "it is pleasing to compare
this sublime enunciation [of pantheistic monism] with
the equally sublime enunciation of the dualistic system
in the sixth *Aeneid*." It is not by such speculative dilettantism that true philosophic poetry is inspired. In fact
we feel altogether more comfortable when we reach the
simple didactic fun of "Sir Hornbook" and "The Round
Table"—the one a short grammar, the other a short
history, in mock-heroics. Here we feel that Peacock is, at
any rate, enjoying himself, and not writing with one or
both eyes on the editor "of some profound review." Even
"Sir Proteus," with its distinctly malicious attacks upon
poets whom he ought to have appreciated, is a relief
after 200 pages of conscientious and unavailing progress
to Parnassus. No doubt it was equally a relief to him.

But the merits of these comical and satirical poems are
merely an earnest of good things to come immediately in
Peacock's prose-fiction; the serious poetry which he pub-

lished before them contains nothing really memorable, and nothing that would have been remembered but for his prose. It is all so lukewarm that it is hard to credit the received opinion that it was during these years that he composed the beautiful "I dug, beneath the cyprus shade, . . ." which ends:

> Frail as thy love, the flowers were dead
> Ere yet the evening sun was set:
> But years shall see the cypress spread,
> Immutable as my regret.

There is, indeed, one published poem—"To Ellen"— which faintly points to such a possibility. But it would be interesting to know the opinion of Peacock's exemplary editors, Mr. Brett-Smith and Mr. Jones, concerning the date of the manuscript poem.

———

8

Proust, Joyce, Forster, and Lawrence

. . . This primary sense of purpose, of which literature is an assertion, though Proust and Joyce have made it a denial, is prior to all its symbolisms, literature itself included. Religion depends upon it, not it upon religion. It is, to use a word of Spengler's, "religiousness" as distinct from religion, which is its symbolism. Without "religiousness" there can be no real religion; but there can be, and to-day are, innumerable religions. But these are, for their cultivated adherents, only conscious "value"-religions, that is, in the true sense, not religions at all. . . . So much the better, it may be thought; one superstition the less. But it is not so simple. There are realities whose reality depends upon whether men experience them: in such a case, obviously, to speak of an exploded superstition is simply a way of saying that the experience of a reality has passed from us. If it be said that, if this were a true reality, it could not have been got rid of, it could be replied that true realities are scarce: he would be a bold man who would enumerate two of them. The category of necessary realities is more helpful. And it seems certain that "religiousness," an indefeasible sense of purpose, is a necessary reality for full human life; that in some form or another it is a *sine quâ non* for the unfolding of human potentialities. A man who is to achieve spiritual greatness must, in some way, believe

Extract from an essay on Spengler's *Decline of the West*. (*Adelphi*, September 1926.)

himself a man with a mission; and he can only do that and remain sane when the mind of society has expectation of men with missions.

This may seem far from Proust and Joyce; in truth it comes very near them. They are men without a mission, without the tension of a vital relation to the world they live in which alone could give their work form and rhythm and progression. The stream of their gifts, rich and abundant, flows out into the sand; in spite of themselves, and in manifest injustice to their own potentialities, they are not artists but *dilettanti*. And this is not simply another version of the often-heard lament that the artist has no genuine function in modern society, which may be true enough; but the dictum puts the blame on society, and leaves the artist free. The truth is otherwise. The lack of purpose and dynamic energy that is in modern society is in the artist also. It is what Chekhov meant when he thought of Tolstoy and said: "*We* are lemonade."

Mr. Lawrence and Mr. Forster stand together because they are in their different ways acutely aware of this condition: Mr. Lawrence as one who feels ever active in himself something which rebels against and would deny it, Mr. Forster less positively, and more intellectually, as one aware of a taint of futility that clings to all his doings with a pen, and, secondly, as one aware of the existence of other conditions of the human consciousness. It is worth musing on the fact (for it is not accidental) that Mr. Forster has written his novel about India, the one continent from which Mr. Lawrence shrank away on his journey round the world. Mr. Lawrence was driven by a positive urge; he was seeking a racial consciousness in which his own could find rest. He sniffed India from Ceylon and went on to Australia. Mr. Forster, from his lack of primary impulse as compared to Mr. Lawrence's, and not from any greater awareness, was proof against Mr. Lawrence's desperate self-deception. He went to India to savour (in no shallow sense) its otherness; not, as Mr. Lawrence would have done, to find a life-stream into which he might plunge and be renewed. Mr. Forster could venture into India safely, knowing himself predestined to be other, as a sort of super-sensitive Indian Civil Servant; Mr. Lawrence could not. For him India might have been really overpowering, and he did not want to be overpowered, but to be renewed; and to be the means of renewing others, to *lead* the way into a new life-consciousness. It may sound preposterous: but that is because everything heroic sounds preposterous nowadays. The only kind of greatness that is not preposterous is the greatness of mere magnitude—the *Great* War, which dynamically was certainly the little one, or Big business; or we may be inclined to allow greatness to achievements in fields of which we know nothing, as in modern physics. But greatness in the things which do nearly concern us is simply preposterous. The vault of the modern universe is like Mr. Forster's cave: it echoes *Oum-Boum* or *Boum-Oum* to all heroics.

Of the four writers we have chosen as significant we may say this: that all of them are significant of the complete absence of religiousness from the modern consciousness, but in different ways, and in ascending progression, thus. Proust unconsciously exhibits it. Joyce exhibits it with a sort of blinkered awareness, limited entirely by his "art"; Forster is genuinely aware of it, to the full capacity of an intellectual awareness; Lawrence is aware of it dynamically, he actually has (by some freak of inheritance) "religiousness" and is in permanent rebellion against a society and an age which has it not. He has even made the attempt to create a new religiousness: only when he finally gives it up will he be welcomed back as the "real artist." Then he will be finished. Take him all in all, Lawrence is the most significant writer we have. His contortions and gropings, which we view with pained surprise, are the index of *our* vacuity. If the sight of him pains us, we should try to remember that it is the spectacle of *us* that frenzies him.

Which does not mean that he is right: merely that he

would be right if we were not all wrong. But it would be easier to get blood out of a stone than a "blood-con-sciousness" out of his contemporaries. He ignores the facts in the same way as those who look back with longing eyes to mediaeval Catholicism. We are lemon-ade, and no contemplative contact with the strong wine of the past will turn us into ardent spirits, nor even into ginger-beer. The backward-looking Renaissance is always a self-deception.

But when I say that we are all wrong, let me not be misunderstood. We are what we are. We cannot even say that the fathers have eaten sour grapes and the chil-dren's teeth are set on edge. Doubtless they did eat them somewhere about Darwin's time: but they ate them, as Darwin did, with the best intentions: and it happened to be the duty of fathers about that time to eat sour grapes, as it is the destiny of children about this time to have their teeth set on edge.

9

English Poetry, 1919

Shall we, or shall we not, be serious? To be serious nowadays is to be ill-mannered, and what, murmurs the cynic, does it matter? We have our opinion; we know that there is a good deal of good poetry in the Georgian book, a little in *Wheels*. We know that there is much bad poetry in the Georgian book, and less in *Wheels*. We know that there is one poem in *Wheels* beside the intense and sombre imagination of which even the good poetry of the Georgian book pales for a moment. We think we know more than this. What does it matter? Pick out the good things, and let the rest go.

And yet, somehow, this question of modern English poetry has become important for us, as important as the war, important in the same way as the war. We can even analogise. *Georgian Poetry* is like the Coalition Government; *Wheels* is like the Radical opposition. Out of the one there issues an indefinable odour of complacent sanctity, an unctuous redolence of *union sacrée*; out of the other, some acidulation of perversity. In the coalition poets we find the larger number of good men, and the larger number of bad ones; in the opposition poets we find no bad ones with the coalition badness, no good ones with the coalition goodness, but in a single case a touch of the apocalyptic, intransigent, passionate hon-

Georgian Poetry, 1918–1919. Edited by E. M. The Poetry Bookshop. *Wheels.* Fourth Cycle. Oxford: B. H. Blackwell (*Athenaeum,* 5 December 1919; reprinted in *Aspects of Literature.*)

esty that is the mark of the martyr of art or life.

On both sides we have the corporate and the individual flavour; on both sides we have those individuals-by-courtesy whose flavour is almost wholly corporate; on both sides the corporate flavour is one that we find intensely disagreeable. In the coalition we find it noxious, in the opposition no worse than irritating. No doubt this is because we recognise a tendency to take the coalition seriously, while the opposition is held to be ridiculous. But both the coalition and the opposition—we use both terms in their corporate sense—are unmistakably the product of the present age. In that sense they are truly representative and complementary each to the other; they are a fair sample of the goodness and badness of the literary epoch in which we live; they are still more remarkable as an index of the complete confusion of aesthetic values that prevails to-day.

The corporate flavour of the coalition is a false simplicity. Of the nineteen poets who compose it there are certain individuals whom we except absolutely from this condemnation, Mr. de la Mare, Mr. Davies, and Mr. Lawrence; there are others who are more or less exempt from it, Mr. Abercrombie, Mr. Sassoon, Mrs. Shove, and Mr. Nichols; and among the rest there are varying degrees of saturation. This false simplicity can be quite subtle. It is compounded of worship of trees and birds and contemporary poets in about equal proportions; it is sicklied over at times with a quite perceptible varnish of modernity, and at other times with what looks to be technical skill, but generally proves to be a fairly clumsy reminiscence of somebody else's technical skill. The negative qualities of this *simplesse* are, however, the most obvious; the poems imbued with it are devoid of any emotional significance whatever. If they have an idea it leaves you with the queer feeling that it is not an idea at all, that it has been defaced, worn smooth by the rippling of innumerable minds. Then, spread in a luminous haze over these compounded elements, is a fundamental right-mindedness; you feel, somehow, that they might have been very wicked, and yet they are very good. There is nothing disturbing about them; *ils peuvent être mis dans toutes les mains*; they are kind, generous, even noble. They sympathise with animate and inanimate nature. They have shining foreheads with big bumps of benevolence, like Flora Casby's father, and one inclines to believe that their eyes must be frequently filmed with an honest tear, if only because their vision is blurred. They are fond of lists of names which never suggest things; they are sparing of similes. If they use them they are careful to see they are not too definite, for a definite simile makes havoc of their constructions, by applying to them a certain test of reality.

But it is impossible to be serious about them. The more stupid of them supply the matter for a good laugh; the more clever the stuff of a more recondite amazement. What *is* one to do when Mr. Monro apostrophises the force of Gravity in such words as these?

> By leave of you man places stone on stone;
> He scatters seed: you are at once the prop
> Among the long roots of his fragile crop
> You manufacture for him, and insure
> House, harvest, implement, and furniture
> And hold them all secure.

We are not surprised to learn further that

> I rest my body on your grass,
> And let my brain repose in you.

All that remains to be said is that Mr. Monro is fond of dogs ('Can you smell the rose?' he says to Dog: 'ah, no!') and inclined to fish—both of which are Georgian inclinations.

Then there is Mr. Drinkwater with the enthusiasm of the just man for moonlit apples—'moon-washed apples of wonder'—and the righteous man's sense of robust rhythm in this chorus from 'Lincoln':

> You who know the tenderness
> Of old men at eve-tide,

> Coming from the hedgerows,
> Coming from the plough,
>   And the wandering caress
> Of winds upon the woodside,
>   When the crying yaffle goes
> Underneath the bough.

Mr. Drinkwater, though he cannot write good doggerel, is a very good man. In this poem he refers to the Sermon on the Mount as 'the words of light From the mountain-way.'

Mr. Squire, who is an infinitely more able writer, would make an excellent subject for a critical investigation into false simplicity. He would repay a very close analysis, for he may deceive the elect in the same way as, we suppose, he deceives himself. His poem 'Rivers' seems to us a very curious example of the *faux bon*. Not only is the idea derivative, but the rhythmical treatment also. Here is Mr. de la Mare:

> Sweet is the music of Arabia
> In my heart, when out of dreams
> I still in the thin clear murk of dawn
> Descry her gliding streams;
> Hear her strange lutes on the green banks
> Ring loud with the grief and delight
> Of the dim-silked, dark-haired musicians
> In the brooding silence of night.
> They haunt me—her lutes and her forests;
> No beauty on earth I see
> But shadowed with that dream recalls
> Her loveliness to me:
> Still eyes look coldly upon me,
> Cold voices whisper and say—
> "He is crazed with the spell of far Arabia,
> They have stolen his wits away."

And here is a verse from Mr. Squire:

> For whatever stream I stand by,
> And whatever river I dream of,
> There is something still in the back of my mind
>   From very far away;

There is something I saw and see not,
A country full of rivers
That stirs in my heart and speaks to me
   More sure, more dear than they.

'And always I ask and wonder
(Though often I do not know)
Why does this water not smell like water?

To leave the question of reminiscence aside, how the delicate vision of Mr. de la Mare has been coarsened, how commonplace his exquisite technique has become in the hands of even a first-rate ability! It remains to be added that Mr. Squire is an amateur of nature,

And skimming, fork-tailed in the evening air,
When man first was, were not the martens
   there?

and a lover of dogs.

   Mr. Shanks, Mr. W. J. Turner, and Mr. Freeman belong to the same order. They have considerable technical accomplishment of the straightforward kind—and no emotional content. One can find examples of the disastrous simile in them all. They are all in their degree pseudo-naïves. Mr. Turner wonders in this way:

It is strange that a little mud
Should echo with sounds, syllables, and letters,
Should rise up and call a mountain Popocatapetl,
And a green-leafed wood Oleander.

Of course Mr. Turner does not really wonder; those four lines are proof positive of that. But what matters is not so much the intrinsic value of the gift as the kindly thought which prompted the giver. Mr. Shanks's speciality is beauty. He also is an amateur of nature. He bids us: 'Hear the loud night-jar spin his pleasant note.' Of course, Mr. Shanks cannot have heard a real night-jar. His description is proof of that. But again, it was a kindly thought. Mr. Freeman is, like Mr. Squire, a more interesting case, deserving detailed analysis. For the moment we can only recommend a comparison of his first

and second poems in this book with 'Sabrina Fair' and
'Love in a Valley' respectively.

It is only when we are confronted with the strange
blend of technical skill and an emotional void that we
begin to hunt for reminiscences. Reminiscences are no
danger to the real poet. He is the splendid borrower who
lends a new significance to that which he takes. He
incorporates his borrowing in the new thing which he
creates; it has its being there and there alone. One can
see the process in the one fine poem in *Wheels*, Mr.
Wilfred Owen's 'Strange Meeting':

> It seemed that out of the battle I escaped
> Down some profound dull tunnel, long since scooped
> Through granites which Titanic wars had groined.
> Yet also there encumbered sleepers groaned,
> Too fast in thought or death to be bestirred.
> Then, as I probed them, one sprang up, and stared
> With piteous recognition in fixed eyes,
> Lifting distressful hands as if to bless.
> And by his smile, I knew that sullen hall.
> With a thousand fears that vision's face was grained;
> Yet no blood reached there from the upper ground,
> And no guns thumped, or down the flues made moan.
> "Strange, friend," I said, "Here is no cause to mourn."
> "None," said the other, "save the undone years,
> The hopelessness. Whatever hope is yours,
> Was my life also"

The poem which begins with these lines is, we believe,
the finest in these two books, both in intention and
achievement. Yet no one can mistake its source. It
comes, almost bodily, from the revised Induction to
'Hyperion.' The sombre imagination, the sombre rhythm
is that of the dying Keats; the creative impulse is that of
Keats.

> None can usurp this height, return'd that shade,
> But those to whom the miseries of the world
> Are misery, and will not let them rest.

That is true, word by word, and line by line, of Wilfred
Owen's 'Strange Meeting.' It touches great poetry by

more than the fringe; even in its technique there is the
hand of the master to be. Those monosyllabic asso-
nances are the discovery of genius. We are persuaded
that this poem by a boy like his great forerunner, who
had the certainty of death in his heart, is the most
magnificent expression of the emotional significance of
the war that has yet been achieved by English poetry. By
including it in his book, the editor of *Wheels* has done a
great service to English letters.

Extravagant words, it may be thought. We appeal to
the documents. Read *Georgian Poetry* and read 'Strange
Meeting.' Compare Wilfred Owen's poem with the very
finest things in the Georgian book—Mr. Davies's 'Lovely
Dames,' or Mr. de la Mare's 'The Tryst,' or 'Fare Well,'
or the twenty opening lines of Mr. Abercrombie's disappointing poem. You will not find those beautiful poems
less beautiful than they are; but you will find in 'Strange
Meeting' an awe, an immensity, an adequacy to that
which has been most profound in the experience of a
generation. You will, finally, have the standard that has
been lost, and the losing of which makes the confusion
of a book like *Georgian Poetry* possible, restored to you.
You will remember three forgotten things—that poetry is
rooted in emotion, and that it grows by the mastery of
emotion, and that its significance finally depends upon
the quality and comprehensiveness of the emotion. You
will recognise that the tricks of the trade have never been
and never will be discovered by which ability can conjure
emptiness into meaning.

It seems hardly worth while to return to *Wheels*.
Once the argument has been pitched on the plane of
'Strange Meeting,' the rest of the contents of the book
become irrelevant. But for the sake of symmetry we will
characterise the corporate flavour of the opposition as
false sophistication. There are the same contemporary
reminiscences. Compare Mr. Osbert Sitwell's *English
Gothic* with Mr. T. S. Eliot's *Sweeney*; and you will
detect a simple mind persuading itself that it has to deal
with the emotions of a complex one. The spectacle is

almost as amusing as that of the similar process in the Georgian book. Nevertheless, in general, the affected sophistication here is, as we have said, merely irritating; while the affected simplicity of the coalition is positively noxious. Miss Edith Sitwell's deliberate painted toys are a great deal better than painted canvas trees and fields, masquerading as real ones. In the poems of Miss Iris Tree a perplexed emotion manages to make its way through a chaotic technique. She represents the solid impulse which lies behind the opposition in general. This impulse she describes, though she is very, very far from making poetry of it, in these not uninteresting verses:

> But since we are mere children of this age,
> And must in curious ways discover salvation
> I will not quit my muddled generation,
> But ever plead for Beauty in this rage.
> Although I know that Nature's bounty yields
> Unto simplicity a beautiful content,
> Only when battle breaks me and my strength is spent
> Will I give back my body to the fields.

There is the opposition. Against the righteous man, the *mauvais sujet*. We sympathise with the *mauvais sujet*. If he is persistent and laborious enough, he may achieve poetry. But he must travel alone. In order to be loyal to your age you must make up your mind what your age is. To be muddled yourself is not loyalty, but treachery, even to a muddled generation.

II Critics

10

Lionel Trilling's *Matthew Arnold*

Mr. Trilling, who is an American professor, has written the best—the most comprehensive and critical—book on Matthew Arnold that exists. It is a little saddening to us that this particular glory should fall to the United States; but there is no doubt that it has so fallen; and we sincerely congratulate the author. That plain duty done, we turn to wondering whether there may not be a reason why it has happened that, although a thoroughly good book on Arnold has been badly needed for a long while, it has been written by an American and not an Englishman. We believe there is a reason: it is that, although Matthew Arnold is always *d'actualité* for any Anglo-Saxon mind, he is a little more actual for the thoughtful American than for the thoughtful Englishman to-day.

The task—"the line"—upon which Matthew Arnold made all his various and eminent gifts converge was the indoctrination of the English people with the necessity of an adequate conception of the State. Malvolio thought nobly of the soul, and in nowise approved the opinion that the soul of our grandam might haply inhabit a bird. Arnold believed that it was just as necessary to think nobly of the State, because the State was the embodiment of the soul of social man. The State would be to the coming democratic society what the soul is to the individual. If it were not so, moral and eventually

Matthew Arnold. By Lionel Trilling. Allen and Unwin. (*Times Literary Supplement,* 11 March 1939.)

material anarchy would ensue. The State was the only conceivable vehicle of what Arnold meant by "culture" when he set before his recalcitrant contemporaries the famous choice between culture and anarchy.

To some extent, in a characteristic half-hearted and grudging fashion, we English have pragmatically accepted the doctrine. We have at least finally and irrevocably abandoned what was once the universal maxim of English politics: that the functions of the State must be reduced to a minimum, and that its positive usefulness was limited to being the strong arm of the Common Law. We are half-way, at least, to the general conviction that the activities of the State may be positive, beneficent and indeed creative. But precisely this is the urgent question in the domestic politics of the United States to-day. Its urgency is compelling an entirely new political alignment; because the time-honoured opposition between Democrat and Republican has no relevance to this issue, just as the opposition between Conservative and Liberal had no relevance to it in Matthew Arnold's day. It is the specific political problem of the Anglo-Saxon peoples, the conquest of whose liberties has been so intimately bound up with religious individualism.

Thus there is a reason why Matthew Arnold should meet with the fullest appreciation from the thoughtful American to-day; and why it has been left for an American critic to grasp, with exemplary clarity, the remarkable unity of Matthew Arnold's thought, and—what is more remarkable still—the unity between his thinking and his life. At the time of his retirement as Inspector of Schools, Arnold said that when he originally took up the position he did so against the grain: he became an inspector simply because he wanted to get married. If it really was so, it is a singular instance of the shaping of man's ends by a divinity, for this was the one position in the inchoate Civil Service of his day which exactly satisfied Arnold's demand upon a conscious man. By entering upon it he united himself with the nascent "stream of tendency," and strove heroically to guide it towards the

good. He devoted his life to a struggle to lay the foundations of an educational system in the grand style, and to
awaken the minds of his countrymen to the necessity of
it. This was the fine and final point of his activity. The
picture of Matthew Arnold, weary with much travelling,
nibbling a bun in lieu of lunch in the classroom of a
dingy Suffolk school, is precious: that is the concrete
reality of civil heroism in an imaginative man.

But what has the inspecting of a "British" school to
do with "the grand style"? Mr. Trilling, at least, is perfectly aware of the connexion. "Whenever Arnold talks
of style," he says excellently, "he is talking about society." For the grand style, as Arnold meant it, is essentially the product of a society which has a style of life,
and lives in accord with a hierarchy of values. In England, for two important centuries, the standard had been
set by a dominant aristocracy. But the social, political
and cultural domination of the English aristocracy was
now at an end, and there was no possibility of halting
the process towards complete democracy. There could be
no social stabilization on the basis of the new industrial
middle class. It would have a temporary preponderance,
but nothing more enduring; and during that temporary
predominance, unless it was newly illuminated, it would
affect the pattern of the aristocracy. But that pattern was
no longer valid, because it was an aristocracy in decline
and no longer a genuine ruling-class. The vices and not
the virtues of an aristocracy would be imitated. It was
impossible to trust to a class any more for the nation's
culture; the building of a new society and the creation of
a new culture must be the work of the classless State of
the future democracy. To educate citizens for that future
society, to lay some foundations of the future State in
the very effort to secure that education—this was to do
all that was humanly possible to guard against the threat
of anarchy, and to prevent "style," in the full meaning of
the word, from perishing.

So bald a summary is singularly inadequate to Matthew Arnold's doctrine; not least because it obscures

Arnold's emphasis on the necessity of continuity. Arnold made no claim to be a systematic thinker; indeed, he made delightful and effective play with the charge that he was not one in the early pages of "Culture and Anarchy." But if he was not a systematic thinker, it was because he was determined to see life whole. To be faithful to the reality—"to keep with the truth," as he put it—his thought had to be sinuous. Mr. Trilling, very justly, lays stress on its dialectical delicacy. The contrast between Arnold's dialectical thinking about society and that which has a monopoly of the epithet to-day is suggestive. It is manifest in Arnold's doctrine of the State. To Marx the State was the instrument of the ruling class; to Arnold it was the embodied morality of a true democracy. The conflict derives from the fact that Marx looked at the existing State in its repressive aspect; whereas Arnold was thinking of a State which did not yet exist and had to be brought into existence if society was to be humane. Arnold, apparently the more idealistic, was the more realistic: for Marx had to look forward to a time when the State should have withered away—a Utopian notion if there ever was one, corollary to the notion that the necessity of morality for the individual would one day disappear. Everybody would be good without having to make an effort. Arnold, on the other hand, was a moralist through and through. He believed that the struggle between the higher and the lower self was the essence of human life. In a moralized, and therefore truly living, society the higher self of society as a whole would be expressed in the dignity and beneficence of the State.

But this everlasting conflict between the higher and the lower selves, which was the condition of life in the individual and in society, Arnold understood dialectically, or, as he would have said, in the light of "the imaginative reason." There was an incessant process of growth at work in the human world. Growth was not to be confused with progress. Because of this process of growth what was at one point of time the higher self of man or society became at a subsequent point a manifestation of the lower self. Thus, for example, the religious individualism of the English seventeenth century, which was then creative, became destructive and anarchical in the nineteenth; so with the respect for individual property, which once had been the necessary guarantee of the person, but now had become, in its acquired sacrosanctity, destructive of personality. Therefore, the true mode of being of the higher self was the "imaginative reason," which could look with lucid interrogation upon these temporary manifestations of man's higher self in the past, and reject them when the virtue had departed from them. The aim of education was the initiation of men into the realm of the imaginative reason. By its operation they could understand that society served another purpose altogether than to protect them in the pursuit of satisfaction for the appetites of their lower selves; it was to enable them to live fully human lives, by strengthening and endorsing the higher self as against the lower.

> His essentially mystic conception of the State [says Mr. Trilling] reads like a Platonic myth. . . . The value of any myth cannot depend upon its demonstrability as a fact, but only on the value of the attitudes it embodies, the further attitudes it engenders and the actions it motivates. In these respects Arnold's myth is still fertile and valuable —and morally inescapable.

Here, for once, Mr. Trilling's insight, though not his sympathy, seems to fail him. He might have paused to consider what is the status of a "morally inescapable myth." If, as it certainly was for Arnold, the moral struggle is the fundamental fact of human life, then it follows that this fundamental fact must be reflected in the nature of society. If the myth is morally inescapable, it is historically inescapable too. "Its failure," says Mr. Trilling, "is the typical liberal failure, for it evades—it was intended to evade—'the crude issue of power.' " But how does it evade this issue? The myth simply declares that society, in order to be finally justified before the imaginative reason, must be moralized; it must encourage and strengthen man's higher self and discourage and weaken his lower self. Such a society may be terribly difficult to achieve, but that is quite different from saying it is inherently impossible to achieve. To say that is, in the last resort, to deny that men can be good. That denial may be valid against those who pin their faith to the "natural goodness" of man. But Arnold was not one of these. Whether or not we like his particular form of the Christian religion, it is evident that he regarded the issue as in the last resort one of Christian belief—and of the power of Christ to regenerate the individual man. Those who oppose Arnold's doctrine of society in the name of Christianity are merely denying the regenerated efficacy of their own religion. Arnold's theory of society is, emphatically, a Christian theory of society.

Mr. Trilling points out the close affinity between Arnold's theory and Rousseau's, to which he does justice; but he makes no mention of the curious fact that there is no evidence that Arnold was directly influenced by Rousseau, or had even read him. If a historical derivation is required for "a morally inescapable myth," Arnold's seems to have arisen, first, from the teachings of his father, and then from his practical investigations into the educational systems of the Continent, where he found the State taking the responsibility for national education in a fashion that was generations ahead of English practice.

If the State were to assume a similar responsibility in the democratic society of England, how could the State be understood? This seems to have been Arnold's approach to the problem; and the practical experience appears to have revivified his father's teaching that the political society in England must be conceived as a developed form of the Christian Church, wherein the Church became the educative instrument of the national society. This was really Coleridge's idea of the "clerisy" adapted to Dr. Arnold's more historical outlook. Matthew Arnold had to adapt it still further, because his father's notion of retaining control of education in the hands of a liberalized national Church had proved impracticable.

It is unusual for a modern critic to do justice to Rousseau; it is positively astonishing to find one doing justice to Dr. Arnold. Mr. Trilling's chapter on Dr. Arnold is quite excellent; as a piece of criticism it is far superior to Mr. Lytton Strachey's amusing but unimaginative essay. Dr. Arnold's sense of historical development, his awareness that society was involved in a process of profound change and his realization that creative action could only proceed from a mind that sought to understand the laws of social change—these were revolutionary novelties in his day; and it is not to be wondered at that, as he grew older, Matthew Arnold spoke of his father with ever-increasing veneration, and more and more found comfort in the thought that he was continuing his father's work, in the spirit if not in the letter. To continue it in the letter was impossible, for Dr. Arnold's basic assumption had failed. The effort to liberalize the Church had caused a reaction towards dogmatism; and the expectation that the Dissenters would conform was disappointed.

Between the two embattled powers of English religion, education was simply neglected. Neither side would accept the aid of the State, for fear of yielding an advantage to the other. It was almost inevitable, in such a situation, that Matthew Arnold should have felt that the cause of education, for its own sake, as the means by which men gained access to the imaginative reason, was the cause of the Christianity of the Kingdom of God. So, in his mind, the order of his father's process was reversed. Through education, he hoped, men would return to Christianity—not the Christianity which they had abandoned, but a Christianity rediscovered and revivified as the substance of what Mr. Trilling calls "the morally inescapable myth" of a democratic society.

Arnold was perhaps inclined to believe this consummation nearer than it has proved to be; but he cannot be called a liberal optimist. Optimism was certainly not natural to him, and his attitude was much rather a hope that the good might prevail, and a determination to do his utmost to that end. And it might very fairly be argued that if Englishmen had listened to him more carefully the situation of Europe would be better than it is. For precisely that which he dreaded happened in 1918–19. The conduct of affairs had fallen from the hands of an aristocracy with a European tradition, and the democracy was not educated enough to behave with a sense of European responsibility.

Whether or not, in his hope of a gradual permeation of society by enlightenment, he evaded "the crude issue of power," it seems pretty plain that those who have been unweary in raising that issue have succeeded much worse than Matthew Arnold; and for a very good reason. People have to be educated even into the necessity of seizing power, and when education into the structure of society gets so far, it has a tendency to go a little farther. As Arnold said, "Criticism must maintain its independence of the practical spirit and its aims." He did not mean that criticism must hold aloof from action. Quite the contrary. He meant that criticism must insist on right action, as distinct from activity busy on immediate results. So he would say that it is not so much more power that the working-class needs to-day as more education; and he would say that the same was true of every other class as well. But not education in the professional sense—education rather into knowledge of their own nature and the society which reflects it. In the light of that understanding, which is spiritual, men know themselves to be members one of another.

A counsel of perfection, perhaps. But we had better take care before we dismiss it as one. Arnold's conviction was that the imaginative reason, awakened in men by education, must lead them to understand the essentially Christian nature of democracy. The working-class ideal, he said to a gathering of London clergymen, is often mixed with all manner of alloy and false notions; yet in itself "it is precious, it is true. And let me observe, it is also the ideal of our religion. It is the business of our religion to make us believe in this very ideal; it is the business of our clergy to profess and to preach it. . . . It is a contracted and insufficient conception of the Gospel which takes into view only the establishment of *righteousness*, and does not also take into view the establishment of the *kingdom*." It is easier, probably, to misunderstand Arnold than to understand him. His zeal for the State did not involve secularization of the Church; it was the evangelization of society which concerned him —a substantial and not a superficial evangelization, in which he called upon the Church to play its part.

Mr. Trilling is critical of Arnold's Christianity. "That Christianity is true: that is, after all, the one thing that Arnold cannot really say." It is surely not so simple as that. Certainly, Arnold would not have replied to the question: "Is Christianity true?" with a simple "Yes." He would have asked, first, what was meant by Christianity. And to that question there are as many answers as there are Christian sects—and more. "The act of translation," says Mr. Trilling further, "which Arnold makes the basis of so much of religious activity is an interesting cultural device, the device of the critic concerned for human continuities." Mr. Trilling forgets that the Church itself has to be concerned for human continuities. The effort of reinterpretation is one to which Arnold's own Church, the Church of England, at least, is committed.

11

William Empson's *Seven Types of Ambiguity*

"To defend analysis in general," says Mr. Empson in the last chapter of his remarkable book, "one has to appeal to the self-esteem of the readers of the analysis, and assume that they possess a quality that is at present much respected." There is a characteristic semblance of humility in this appeal to the elect, before which we are compelled to capitulate. We hasten to take refuge in the asylum which Mr. Empson has deliberately prepared for us, by his polite indication that the now respected quality may not be respected for ever; for, alas! we are painfully conscious of not possessing it. We can only plead a genuine, if unintelligent, interest in a person who possesses it so abundantly, indeed so alarmingly, as Mr. Empson. Therefore we gather up gratefully his subsequent hints.

> This quality is admired at present because it gives one a certain power of dealing with anything that may turn out to be true; since the War people have felt that that may be absolutely anything; I do not say that this power is of unique value; it tends to prevent the sensibility from having its proper irrigating and fertilizing effect upon the person as a whole; a medieval sensibility may have been more total and satisfying than a modern one. But it is widely and reasonably felt that those people are better able to deal with our present difficulties whose defences

Seven Types of Ambiguity. By William Empson. Chatto and Windus. (*Times Literary Supplement*, 18 December 1930.)

are strong enough for them to be able to afford to understand things; nor can I conceal my sympathy with those who want to understand as many things as possible, and to hang those consequences which cannot be foreseen.

The thing which Mr. Empson especially sets himself to understand is poetry. His defences, by implication, are strong enough for him to be able to afford to understand it; and his conviction is patent that it can be understood. "The reasons that make a line of verse likely to give pleasure, I believe, are like the reasons for anything else; one can reason about them."

With Mr. Empson reasons are plentiful as blackberries. The staple of his method is to set out in swift succession all possible meanings of the verse fragments which he chiefly selects for his exhibits, and tacitly to invite our consideration, first, of the probability that all these meanings were in various degrees present to the mind of the poet, and secondly, of the desirability that all these meanings should be present (again in various degrees) to our minds as readers in order that we should fully appreciate the poetry before us. That is the simplest account we can give of the method. To give a really characteristic example of it in operation would, for obvious reasons, be too great a tax upon our space. The method has at least one merit. It emphasizes the simple but none the less easily neglected fact that comparatively little poetry, when submitted to rigorous grammatical and logical analysis, is unambiguous. Ambiguity, in the wide and generous sense in which Mr. Empson uses the word, is almost essential to poetry. The disturbing question, for one lacking in the respected quality of love of analysis for its own sake, is whether we gain, and what and how much we gain, by submitting the admitted ambiguity of poetry to this rigorous analysis.

Among the poems which Mr. Empson submits to treatment are the beautiful verses of George Herbert on the Crucifixion. The analysis occupies more than eight pages. We detach a portion of his comment on the last verse:

> But now I die; Now, all is finished.
> My woe, man's weal; and now I bow my head:
> Only let others say, when I am dead,
>   Never was grief like mine.

This, for Mr. Empson, is riddled with ambiguity, which he thus unfolds:

> One must consider that he may *bow his head* in submission or because he is biding his time; that *now* may mean: "I have attained the promised rest," or "You have lost your last chance of treating me properly"; that *weal*, which claims here to mean prosperity, carries some trace of its other meaning at that time, not a scar but a pustule; . . . and that English has no clear form for the Oratio Obliqua. He may wish, therefore, that his own grief may never be exceeded among the humanity he pities, "After the death of Christ, may there never be a grief like Christ's"; he may, incidentally, wish that they may *say* this, that he may be sure of recognition, and of a church that will be a soundingboard to his agony; or he may mean *mine* as a quotation from the *others*, "Only let there *be* a retribution, only let my torturers say never was grief like theirs, in the day when my agony shall be exceeded."
>
> I am not sure how far people would be willing to accept this double meaning; I am only sure that after you have once apprehended it . . . you will never be able to read the poem without remembering that it is a possibility.

That it is, in the abstract, a possible meaning, we may admit. But we must insist that the effort of abstraction by which this meaning becomes possible is altogether unnatural. It assumes a complete ignorance of the story of the Passion, as though Herbert's poem might conceivably be read by some dispassionate inhabitant of Mars. It could occur to one who had felt the beauty and pathos of the poem, only after a deliberate and violent effort to forget the poem as a poem. And if it is true, as Mr. Empson says, that once you have apprehended this possible meaning, you will never be able to read the poem without remembering the possibility, it follows that you have, by giving this licence to your appetite for analysis, actually to some extent destroyed your capacity of response to the poem as poem. For after all, a poem is a poem not least by virtue of its power to ward off these vagaries of the intellect. It is to some degree an incantation, a word of immediate power, compelling the wandering mind to response of a certain order; and only so far as the receiving mind restrains its speculations within the limits of this order is it speculating about the poem at all. For, paradoxical though it must sound, the poem and the words which compose the poem are not the same thing, by the same necessity that an organic whole is not the same thing as the sum of its parts.

This simple truth is not acceptable to analysis. Not that we suppose that Mr. Empson, as a person, would object to it; but Mr. Empson, as analyst, must for ever be straining to deny it. He is, to do him justice, aware of the difficulty. Speaking of the analytical critic, he says:

> They must have the power of reacting to a poem sensitively and definitely and then, having fixed the reaction, properly stained on a slide, they must be able to turn the microscope on to it with a certain indifference and without smudging it with their fingers.

Theoretically, that is excellent; but in practice it happens otherwise. In the comment upon George Herbert's poem, for instance, it is not the reaction to the poem which is being examined, but the words of the poem. And the words of the poem are the cause of the reaction to the poem only in so far as their possible meanings are circumscribed and governed by the reaction to the poem as a whole. Unless analysis observes this inward humility, it becomes incontinent; it not only brings us no nearer, but definitely takes us away from the goal of more intimate understanding.

The total effect of Mr. Empson's book is of this kind. It is incontinent, and it obscures rather than explains. It is the work of an exceedingly able young man, who has not learned to control his abilities, and perhaps sees no reason why he should control them. One has the impression that he has been turned, or has turned himself, loose on to poetry; and that poetry has no particular importance to him save as an opportunity for a free exercise of his abilities.

12

F. R. Leavis's *D. H. Lawrence: Novelist*

Dr. Leavis's study of D. H. Lawrence's novels opens with the words: "This book carries on from *The Great Tradition*." Readers of that book will regard the statement as something of a warning. For the treatment of the novelists dealt with in it was highly selective. Dickens barely scraped his second class, and that solely on the strength of *Hard Times*. And only portions of the three placed in the first class—George Eliot, James and Conrad—were awarded highest honours.

Lawrence is now admitted among them, and only Lawrence among their successors. But his entry is triumphal. Though Dr. Leavis does not say so in so many words, from his tone it is evident that he regards him as the greatest of them all. Never has he been so prodigal of eulogy; never quite so pugnacious in downing the opposition, which consists, for Dr. Leavis, not only of those who have been in any way publicly critical of Lawrence's work but even of the novelists who have had the misfortune to be contemporary with him.

Nevertheless, he applies to Lawrence the same selective method. One hundred pages of his book are devoted to *The Rainbow* and *Women in Love*; another fifty to *St. Mawr* and *The Captain's Doll*; and since, excluding two appendices, there are only 300 in all, and many of these are spent on unnecessary polemic, the treatment of

F. R. Leavis: *D. H. Lawrence: Novelist*. Chatto and Windus. (*Times Literary Supplement*, 28 October 1955.)

the rest of Lawrence's prose fiction is distinctly eclectic. Dr. Leavis has his defence. "I want the stress to fall unambiguously on *The Rainbow, Women in Love,* and the tales." These two novels, according to him, are of a much higher order than the others which Lawrence wrote; and they have had "essentially no recognition at all." But they are, in fact, the "supreme creative achievement" in "the great tradition" of the English novelists since Jane Austen, who are "the successors of Shakespeare."

It is a thankless task to criticize such enthusiasm; but in the interest of a just appreciation of one who, taken all in all, is the most significant English writer of the twentieth century, a caveat must be entered. Lawrence can be made to fit into "the great tradition" of the English novel, as Dr. Leavis understands it, only by a great deal of manipulation. Take, for instance, *The Rainbow.* Concerning the earlier part of it, Dr. Leavis has much that is wise and illuminating to say; he makes just and revealing comparisons to Lawrence's advantage with George Eliot. But when he comes to deal with the later and more baffling part of the book—the story of the relations between Ursula and Anton—he passes hurriedly over it.

> A more serious criticism, perhaps, bears on the signs of too great a tentativeness in the development and organization of the later part; signs of a growing sense in the writer of an absence of any conclusion in view. Things very striking in themselves haven't as clear a function as they ought to have. Above all, the sterile deadlock between Ursula and Skrebensky—a theme calling, we can see, for the developments it gets in *Women in Love,* but cannot have here—seems too long drawn out.

Considering the importance of this relation between Ursula and Anton, Dr. Leavis's perfunctory treatment of it amounts to evasion. For the difficulty is not that the sterile deadlock is too long drawn out, but it is presented in terms which, even to eager and sympathetic readers, are incomprehensible. It may be that what is arcane to them is lucid to Dr. Leavis. But if ever exegesis was required, it is surely here. What is it that happens in the scene in the stackyard in Chapter XI, or on the seashore in Chapter XV? We have Lawrence's word for it that Ursula apparently unwittingly became for Anton "the darkness, the challenge, the horror"; that she "consumed and annihilated" him and that the annihilation was permanent; but the process by which it was accomplished, though described in detail and with vehemence by Lawrence; remains entirely mysterious. Yet this is the major psychological or spiritual happening in the second half of *The Rainbow*. Dr. Leavis does not explain it at all.

Neither does he do so in his detailed exposition of *Women in Love*. In that novel, the theme of Ursula's destructive relation to Skrebensky is taken up again in the relation of Gudrun and Gerald; while Ursula finds a man whom she cannot annihilate and to whom she must surrender, in Rupert. Lawrence's descriptions of the crucial moments in both relations are as mysterious as they were when the book was first published. Again Dr. Leavis passes them over: this time not quite in silence, for he quotes one of them and comments:

> I see here a fault of which I could find worse examples in *Women in Love*, though it is a fault that I do not now see as bulking so large in the book as I used to see it. It seems to me that in these places Lawrence betrays by an insistent and over-emphatic explicitness, running at times to something one can only call jargon, that he is uncertain —uncertain of the value of what he offers; uncertain whether he really holds it—whether a valid communication has really been defined and conveyed in terms of his creative art.

That is all. The difficulty is dismissed. But it has not been overcome. Consequently Dr. Leavis gives the impression of expounding and exalting a different novel from that which Lawrence actually wrote: a version bowdlerized, or at least mitigated *in usum Delphini*.

It is easy enough to understand Lawrence's intention in *Women in Love*: to present first the contrast between a man who immolates himself to the mechanism of modern civilization and one who is in dynamic revolt against it; and also to present the fatal influence on the man-woman relation of the inward sterility of Gerald, and the gleam of hope in the "love" that is based on Ursula's response to the vitality with which Birkin conquers his own despair. The theme is profound and prophetic. But much of its working out is mysterious. Again we ask what it is that happens in the crucial scene where Ursula enters into the "full mystic knowledge" of Birkin's "suave loins of darkness." If it is true, as Dr. Leavis suggests, that Lawrence was uncertain of the value of what he offered, uncertain whether he really held it, it has a vital bearing on the convincingness of the novel: for Ursula's relation to Birkin is certainly offered as the way out of the spiritual impasse of contemporary civilization. It is presented as "normative," to use Dr. Leavis's word.

Dr. Leavis's method of isolating the two novels from their important context does real injustice to Lawrence's achievement: for the subsequent novels are full of implicit and explicit criticism of what he had previously "offered," or at least of readjustment of it to further experience. So that to dispose of the subsequent novels as a preliminary to the consideration of the two that preceded them seems, in the literal sense of the word, preposterous. It is as a whole—as the unique record, and imaginative projection of the life and thought adventure of a man prophetically sensitive to the deep inward decay of a civilization—that Lawrence's achievement is so astonishing. It is at once greater and less than Dr. Leavis represents it. He is understandably indignant with those who merely allow Lawrence a certain magic of style; but in his effort to vindicate for him the position of the supreme artist—let us put it bluntly, since Dr. Leavis plainly implies it—of the same order as Shakespeare, he unduly exaggerates the perfection of some, and unduly depreciates the merit of other of Lawrence's work. Thus he dismisses *The Plumed Serpent* as "a bad book and a regrettable performance." Even if that were a sound judgment (as it is not) the phenomenon would call for explanation, for there is no doubt that Lawrence himself considered it as serious an undertaking as any novel he ever wrote.

Of his contrary tendency to impute perfection to work with serious defects his extreme eulogy of *St. Mawr* is a striking example. *St. Mawr*, it will be remembered, is the story of how a stallion comes to reveal to a woman the utter insufficiency of her husband and her marriage, and the sterility of the polite semi-artistic world in which her life has been caught. Lou, in contemplating the stallion, receives a revelation of the reality of the life-power that has been suppressed and destroyed in men of the modern civilization, and she imagines a "new man" in whom the vivid instinctive life of the animal should be completed by a kindred swift intelligence. Dr. Leavis admits that this ideal is not presented in any character of the story.

> But it is, nevertheless, irresistibly present in *St. Mawr* the dramatic poem; it is no mere abstract postulate. It is present as the marvellous creative intelligence of the author.

Is this argument more than ingenious? Can an author's intelligence, however creative and pervasive, really take the place of a created character of the kind posited? From *The White Peacock* onward Lawrence made many attempts to present such a character, the last being Mellors in *Lady Chatterley's Lover*. But, significantly, none of them has Dr. Leavis's approval. So he subtly, and perhaps unconsciously, shifts his ground. Lou repudiates her mother's cynical insinuation that she wants a cave man.

> He's a brute, a degenerate. A pure animal man would be as lovely as a deer or a leopard, burning like a flame fed straight from underneath. And he'd be part of the unseen, like a mouse is, even. And he'd never cease to wonder,

he'd breathe silence and unseen wonder, as the partridges do, running in the stubble. . . . Ah no, mother, I want the wonder back again, or I shall die.

On which Dr. Leavis comments:

> Lawrence can make "wonder" . . . seem so much more than a vaguely recoiling romanticism, because for him it is so much more. He can affirm with a power not given to poor Lou, who is not a genius, and there is nothing merely postulated about the positives he affirms.
>
> The power of the affirmation lies, not in any insistence or assertion or argument but in the creative fact, his art; it is that which is an irrefutable witness. What his art *does* is beyond argument or doubt. It is not a question of metaphysics or theology. . . . Great art, something created and *there*, is what Lawrence gives us. And there we undeniably *have* a world of wonder and reverence, where life wells up from mysterious springs.

For all its surface plausibility, this burkes the real issue. In so far as it is relevant to Lou's demand for a "new man," it amounts to no more than implying that Lawrence himself was such a man. And Lawrence himself, in a remarkable sequence of novels with which Dr. Leavis does not really grapple, dealt with astonishing honesty with that possibility, or hypothesis, and demonstrated where it failed. The wonder, which Lawrence the writer felt and so marvellously communicated, of the animal and natural world, does not extend to the human being—except in the case of his fictional presentation of himself.

But that, it might be said, is because the "wonder" is not in civilized man or woman. It has departed. That assuredly was Lawrence's conviction. But Dr. Leavis does not adopt it. Instead he asserts that such figures as Rico and Mrs. Witt are triumphs of creative art. Surely he is hypnotizing himself. He is apparently not quite unaware of the danger.

> Lou's vision is of a flood of evil enveloping the world. Rico "being an artist," and bent on kudos and "fun," might seem to be too much of a figure of comedy to play the major part assigned to him in so portentous a vision. It

is a mark of the wonderful success of the tale in its larger intention that, irresistible as it is in its comedy, we are not moved to anything like that criticism: the significance represented by the visionary role inheres potently in the Rico we have been made to realize. He is, in the first place, we may say, Bloomsbury.

A half-page of denunciation follows. A sense of anti-climax is irrepressible. Whether or not Rico is a plausible embodiment of Bloomsbury—and one would say he was not—he cannot carry the weight of apocalyptic significance with which Dr. Leavis would invest him; neither can Mrs. Witt, with her enjoyment of the churchyard, carry hers. With characteristic gravity Dr. Leavis warns us:

> Mrs. Witt's note is not so much merely light as it sounds. The churchyard, with its funerals, becomes an insistent theme. It isn't, for Mrs. Witt, an obsession with death as the terrifying and inescapable reality, but a fear that death will prove unreal. Reported in this way, the case may not seem to carry much in the way of convincing poignancy. But this is what we are actually given; the thing is *done*, in its inevitability an astonishing triumph of genius; and since the success—the convincing transmutation, in Mrs. Witt, of hard-boiled ironic destructiveness into agonized despair—is crucial to the success of the whole, a long quotation will be in place.

The long quotation cannot be copied; but to the present writer's sense it simply does not substantiate Dr. Leavis's claim. And the shrillness of his superlatives which culminate in the dictum that "one would have said that the kind of thing hadn't been done and couldn't be done, outside Shakespearian dramatic poetry" seems to be a means of drowning the still small voice of critical sanity.

St. Mawr is a significant story; but not a supreme one. Dr. Leavis's criticism of it has been dealt with in some detail, because his method of intense and highly selective concentration on parts of Lawrence's prose fiction admits no other mode of questioning. To account for his aberration—and his emphatic endorsement of Rico as a convincing apocalyptic character can be reckoned no less

—we should invoke his unnecessary divagation against Bloomsbury, and his previous invective against the successors of Bloomsbury.

In the period in which Auden was so rapidly established as a major poet and remained one for so long, and Spender became overnight the modern Shelley, it was not to be expected that the portrayer of Rico would receive the sympathetic attention denied him in the emancipated twenties.

Dr. Leavis has, in fact, made Rico a symbol of his critical detestations. Rico's illusory magnitude and convincingness as a character are a function of his own private universe. They are not intrinsic to the character presented by Lawrence. Here we touch upon a real and pervasive weakness of Dr. Leavis's championship of Lawrence. For all his genuine reverence for Lawrence's genius, he cannot refrain from using him as a weapon of offence against those whom he regards as literary enemies. What in Lawrence himself was lighthearted becomes weighted with a deadly seriousness in Dr. Leavis's commentary: Lawrence's casual dismissals are transmuted into excommunications.

It is an exaggeration to represent Lawrence as neglected since his death. He has been continually in the consciousness and on the conscience of literate England for at least twenty-five years. And if he has not yet been accepted as the only inheritor of "the great tradition" of the English novel, it is largely because he was, essentially, something more important than that—more revolutionary, more truly new, more challenging, more disturbing—which refuses to be accommodated in our conventional categories. Dr. Leavis, by virtue of his profession, has made a heroic effort to subsume all that he can of this unique being under the category of "supreme artistic intelligence." He has made a brave and stimulating effort to separate Lawrence's art from his doctrine; but in order to do it he has been compelled to a tacit expurgation. The doctrine is always there.

13

E. M. W. Tillyard and C. S. Lewis's
The Personal Heresy

One cannot help smiling a little at the remark with which Mr. Lewis concludes his second paper. "We have both learnt our dialectic," he assures Dr. Tillyard, "in the rough academic arena where knocks that would frighten the London literary coteries are given and taken in good part." The implication is double-edged: to some it may suggest (as doubtless it was intended to suggest) that here we are invited to witness a real critical struggle —a kind of all-in wrestling instead of the namby-pamby business that prevails in the metropolis; to others it may suggest that the contest is of the kind that all-in wrestling is generally reputed to be—"full of sound and fury, signifying nothing"—but good entertainment, nevertheless, for those who are not over-nice.

Entertainment rather than enlightenment is, we think, the chief outcome of this debate between Mr. Lewis and Dr. Tillyard on "The Personal Heresy." In the first place it is not very easy to grasp what exactly "the personal heresy" is supposed to be, or who holds it. The phrase is Mr. Lewis's, and it served originally as the title of an essay in which Dr. Tillyard, Mr. Eliot, Mr. Hugh Kingsmill and Professor Garrod—who must have been rather surprised to find themselves in the pillory

The Personal Heresy: A Controversy. By E. M. W. Tillyard and C. S. Lewis. Oxford University Press; London: Milford. (*Times Literary Supplement*, 29 April 1939.)

together—were exhibited as showing more or less aggra-
vated symptoms of the heresy. In response to Dr. Tillyard's objection, Mr. Lewis admits that his enemy is
"much less a fully fledged theory than a half-conscious
assumption which I saw creeping into critical tradition
under the protection of its very vagueness." The assumption—at least as old as Dryden—is that in reading a work
of literature the reader makes contact with the "personality" of the author. Mr. Lewis proposes to blow this
vague theory out of the water.

But in this form the theory is too vague either to be
asserted or denied. Accordingly Mr. Lewis makes it more
definite, and undertakes first to show that "there is at
least one very obvious sense in which it is certain that
the object offered to us by a good poem is not the poet's
personality." Mr. Lewis makes short work of that. But
such a position, if held at all, is held by few. What is
generally implied in the statement, which is fairly frequently made or suggested, that a writer's work is an
expression or a revelation of his personality, is exactly
what is implied in Flaubert's well-known definition of
style: "Le style, c'est une manière de voir."

That is to say, that in good literature, or writing that
has the quality of style, the reader is enabled to share the
author's particular vision of the things which he contem-
plates in imagination. That this vision is particular and
unique, and is in some intelligible and important sense a
faculty of the author's personality, is the position which
Mr. Lewis has to demolish. He achieves nothing to his
purpose by refuting such a very strange and unfamiliar
assertion as that, when we read poetry, we have before us
"a representation which claims to be the poet."

Against the larger and more fundamental position Mr.
Lewis brings no argument at all. On the contrary he
accepts it, or appears to do so. After quoting, "When as
in silks my Julia goes . . ." and insisting for a space that
the poem is about silk—though surely, as Dr. Tillyard
objects, it is at least about Julia as well—and not about
Herrick, he continues:

It may be true that what I am aware of in reading Herrick's poem is silk, but it is not silk as an object *in rerum natura*. I see it as Herrick saw it; and in so doing, it may be argued, I do come into contact with his temperament in the most intimate—perhaps in the only possible way. For the moment I not only accept but embrace this view of the matter.

If that is indeed the case, there seems to be nothing left to argue about. For the conclusion seems unavoidable that through a writer's works as a whole the sensitive reader attains a contact with a writer's temperament more intimate than can be achieved in any other way. Mr. Lewis does not deny this: but he seems concerned to maintain that it is quite unimportant or irrelevant to poetry. He is willing (he says) to speak of "the Racinity of Racine and the Shakespeareanity of Shakespeare"; but "let us remember that their poethood consists not in the fact that each approached the universal world from their own angle (all men do that), but in their power of telling us what things are severally to be seen from those angles." The reminder is pertinent, but surely exaggerated. All men may indeed "approach" the universal world from their own angle, but it is doubtful indeed whether all men "see" it. Wordsworth's account would seem to be nearer the truth:

> Oh! many are the Poets that are sown
> By nature; men endowed with highest gifts,
> The vision and the faculty divine;
> Yet wanting the accomplishment of verse

"Many," but few in comparison with the total of mankind. In any case, the fact that the differentia of the poet consists in his power of utterance does not in the least diminish the importance, or the relevance to poetry, of what he utters. Because the specific achievement of the poet is utterance, it does not follow, as Mr. Lewis says it does, that "he does not express his personality." Everything depends on the meaning of such a phrase; and the now general substitution of the notion of "expression" for the ancient notion of "imitation" cannot be remedied simply by interpreting "expression" in the sense of "imitation." When it is maintained that a writer "expresses" his personality, it is not being asserted that he "imitates" his personality, in the Aristotelian sense of "mimēsis," but that he conveys or communicates his personality—his own distinctive "way of seeing," and feeling, and thinking. By what other means could he achieve the desideratum posited by a critic so immune from any suspicion of the "personal heresy" as Johnson —namely, to make strange things familiar and familiar things strange?

A writer's distinctive mode of seeing and feeling and thinking is the main component of his personality, at any rate in the sense in which that word can profitably be used as a term of literary criticism. To suggest, as Mr. Lewis does, that the personality is merely something like a window through which the writer looks upon the world, is to create an unnecessary and insoluble problem by enforcing a cleavage, tolerable only to abstract episte-mology, between the subject and the object. Goethe's was a much saner and less pedantic view when he main-tained that the artist—in his respect merely a type of man—discovers himself by discovering the world. To argue that self-expression is quite distinct from express-ing (or imitating) the objective world is to fly in the face of experience. A pure self-expression, conceived as a proc-ess entirely other than an expression of a world of ob-jects, is a chimera; no less chimerical is a poetic imitation of a world of objects which is unaccompanied by self-ex-pression—the "poetless poetry," after which Mr. Lewis seems to hanker.

A cause of incessant confusion in the discussion is the vagueness of the notion of personality; and we cannot help thinking that the debate would have been far more profitable had it developed into a discussion of the meaning of the word. As used by Mr. Lewis the word "personality" appears approximately to mean the total behaviour of any human being: "personality" is therefore something which is common to all men and in the same degree, and it is difficult to see what meaning Mr. Lewis would attach, for example, to the notion of one man's personality being richer than another's.

For Dr. Tillyard, on the other hand, personality is something quite other than the purely metaphysical uniqueness which inheres in every man by virtue of his mere existence. "By 'personality' or 'normal personality' I mean some mental pattern which makes Keats Keats and not Mr. Smith or Mr. Jones." At another time he speaks of it as "the poet's characteristic, unmistakable self," which (he says) is the more likely to be revealed if the poet has experienced, in the composition of his work, an entire forgetfulness of self. This is a slightly different conception from the former one of "the mental pattern"; and it would have been helpful if Dr. Tillyard had made some use of Mr. Herbert Read's interesting discussion of personality as a critical concept. Yet a third notion of personality seems to be on the point of emerging in the sentence: "When then we talk of the poetry of Milton or of Wordsworth being more personal than that of Shakespeare or of Keats we may be meaning that it expresses a more austerely rigid nature." This is, of course, allied to Keats's distinction between the man of Character (that is, the man with a developed *persona*, in Dr. Jung's sense) and the man of Genius; or between his own "selfless" poetic nature and Wordsworth's "egotistical sublime."

But, manifestly, when the content of the word "personality" is so fluid, and no preliminary or eventual agreement is reached concerning the meaning to be attached to it, no very positive conclusion can be reached at the end of 150 pages of discussion. We gather that Dr. Tillyard is unrepentant for his participation in "the personal heresy"; but we remain in our original condition of uncertainty as to what "the personal heresy" is. What Mr. Lewis appears to be hunting down under this description is the tendency of the romantic poets to exalt the poet as a superior human being, as the man *par excellence.* That tendency was certainly marked in our English romantic poets; and just as certainly it was due to the decay of religion. In order to justify his own activity as a poet, and the dedication of his life to that activity, the Romantic poet was compelled to conceive of himself as a poet-prophet.

No doubt it is a dangerous rôle to assume; but on the other hand it must be admitted that the great English romantic poets were singularly restrained. They thought highly of themselves—and posterity has come to agree with them—but they did not behave extravagantly. What is too easily forgotten is that, if they had not been sustained by a tremendous belief in themselves and a very exalted conception of their function, they could hardly have carried on at all; for they were all very unpopular. This combination of circumstances was peculiar. One consequence was that these, our second constellation of great poets, were definitely more "personal" than their great predecessors. They did not write for a prepared audience, they had no recognized status in the social order, they were the product of a society in a process of revolutionary change; and not the least part of their effort was to establish themselves as persons in a society in which the old order had collapsed.

It is desirable to distinguish between the new emphasis on personality which was necessary to poets of such a kind at such a period, when poets could continue to be poets only at the cost of a considerable personal struggle, when, in fact, the poet was compelled to be something of a hero, and the personality which is inseparable from any conspicuous achievement of style in literature. The most objective, the most studiously impersonal of writers, if he achieves "magic of style," indubitably communicates his personality in some important meaning of that word. If we were to take Mr. Lewis's arguments seriously it would be nonsense to speak, for example, of the personality of Virgil; but, in fact, it is the most natural thing in the world. "Le style, c'est l'homme même," said Buffon. That is not a philosophical proposition; but it has been felt by many to contain the essential truth of the matter.

The more perplexing question is to determine how far elaborate biographical details—which would supply the main elements of any picture of a "personality" according to Mr. Lewis's use of the word—have any valuable illumination to throw upon the personality revealed in a writer's work. Suppose we possessed the kind of information concerning Shakespeare which in our unregenerate moments we sometimes desire—an intimate personal diary for a period of twenty years—we might be the richer for a diary, but we should almost certainly be the poorer by the whole of Shakespeare's works. To write the kind of diary which would be truly illuminating Shakespeare would have had to devote to it the energy which made his plays.

In so far, then, as Mr. Lewis is engaged in protesting against a modern tendency to substitute biography for critical appreciation, and gossip for judgment, the protest is welcome enough. But even within this limited field it seems that he has partly mistaken the quarry. The prevailing extravagant appetite for the "personal," for which a competitive journalism is compelled to cater, is surely to be explained as a kind of psychological compensation for the serious and increasing diminution of truly personal relations in a mechanical and competitive society. The "depersonalization of social relations" which Wordsworth observed and deplored more than a hundred years ago has continued ever since; and the process has vastly accelerated, so that even a man of fifty to-day can look back on the social relations of his childhood—the sense of neighbourhood—almost as belonging to another world.

If to supply the deficiency in true sociality we make friends of the illustrious dead, it would seem to be the least harmful form of compensation—and one perhaps which it is ungracious of a Fellow of an Oxford college to deplore. It is hardly decorous for a member of one of the few surviving forms of social society to object to "attention to Shakespeare's personality," as revealed in his works, on the ground that "it is a misdirection of feelings properly social and active to an object which admits of no action and no true society." The proposition is disputable in itself, and, if insisted on would make havoc of attitudes even more precious, and much more universal, than a sense of intimacy with Shakespeare's "comprehensive soul."

14

H. G. Wells's *The Fate of Homo Sapiens*

Mr. H. G. Wells has written a brave book. It might have been just as brave and a good deal more inspiring if he had been more tender of men's religious susceptibilities; but his trampling on these with a heavy hoof must not blind us to the fact that the book is a brave one. Perhaps it is the bravery of desperation; but if Mr. Wells is deeply convinced that the situation of mankind is desperate, shall he not proclaim it? If he believes that the religions—all the religions—are merely so many veils interposed between men's eyes and the truth, is he not to say so? We think it is far better than he should have spoken his mind fully as he has done than pretend to an unction that is unnatural to him. He has no sympathy whatever with any religious or metaphysical view of the world; and he has no understanding of either.

His title—"The Fate of Homo Sapiens"—indicates the angle of his approach: it is biological and ecological. He says in his concluding chapter:

> There is no reason whatever to believe that the order of nature has any greater bias in favour of man than it had in favour of the icthyosaur or the pterodactyl. In spite of all my disposition to a brave-looking optimism, I perceive that now the universe is bored with him, is turning a hard face to him, and I see him being carried less and less intelligently and more and more rapidly, suffering as every

The Fate of Homo Sapiens. By H. G. Wells. Secker and Warburg. (*Times Literary Supplement*, 5 August 1939.)

ill-adapted creature must suffer in gross and detail, along the stream of fate to degradation, suffering and death.

There is nothing profoundly original in the broad diagnosis from which this despair proceeds. Two main factors in the present situation are acknowledged by anyone whose mind is accustomed to the biological and evolutionary view of human history. The first is that within a space of time incredibly short compared with the evolutionary history of man, invention and science have completely changed the material environment of human life. Mr. Wells impresses upon us the nature of the change when he says that the total physical energy employed in a day of the life of Elizabethan England amounted to much less than that which is consumed today in running the lighting and the transport alone of a single city like Kansas City or Manchester; more vividly still, he suggests that all the physical energy expended in the battle of Agincourt is less than that liberated in a single high-explosive shell. The energy which mankind has, not under its control—far from it—but at its disposal to-day is, compared to what it possessed two hundred years ago, truly tremendous. The power of the human species to create or destroy has been multiplied ten thousand times.

The second main factor is the frighteningly small change in the mental and spiritual habits of the creatures to whom this colossal material change has occurred. The old habits of thought, the ancient prejudices, once adequate to an economy which allowed precious little margin of energy over and above what was strictly necessary for cultivating the earth and keeping the race alive, persist almost unchanged. In Mr. Wells's deceptive language, "the existing mental organization of our species is entirely insufficient to control the present situation, which nevertheless might, with an adequate effort, be controlled." The third factor, the emphasis on which is new to us in such an analysis, is the "disruptive driving force of an excess of bored and unemployed young men, which must in some manner find relief, or it will probably shatter human life altogether under the new conditions." This last factor is not quite on a parity with the other two, because the existence of such a mass of young men is manifestly the outcome of the second factor. If *Homo sapiens*, congregated into societies, had achieved a "mental organization" adequate to his new situation, the millions of young men at a loose end would not exist to be either an insoluble social problem in the "democratic," or the main components of vast aggressive armies in the totalitarian, states. Those hordes of bored and baffled young men are the concrete and living embodiment of the superabundance of energy now at human disposal; they are part of that surplus and wasted energy in a particular form: but they are not of course the whole of it—all the incredible expenditure of energy in the constructive destruction which is armaments-production belongs to the same category.

Still, we may admit the urgency of what Mr. Wells calls "the Youth Pressure theme"; and it is probably true that in practical political terms (which are assuredly not terms of "practical politics") the crux of the situation is the application of an educational revolution to the youth of the present world. But how are they to be taught to understand the human situation? In an increasingly large section of the world the opportunities of free investigation are positively denied to youth; and in those countries where education is still in some sense free it cannot be said that the comprehensive vision is encouraged. And it seems to us that Mr. Wells is still very romantic, in his own peculiar fashion, when he allows himself to dream of the institution in America of a kind of super-university to instruct the world, and youth in particular, into the realities.

> If only this absolute necessity for an organized World-Brain, a gigantic but still possible super-university, set above all these admirable, but ineffective scattered foundations to utilize and consolidate them, if only that could fire the imagination of a few energetic spirits; then the whole outlook of the human species might be changed.

But is not this a kind of intellectual gigantism? Are not the vital facts of the situation simple? And are they not—in themselves—as capable of being expounded to an adherent of the numerous religions which Mr. Wells so wholeheartedly condemns as to any adept of his own brand of atheism? Some people at least find no difficulty in reconciling a biological approach to the problem of man's terrestrial destiny with the profession of Christianity. The difficulties in the way of creating a universal awareness are tremendous enough without insisting on the prior necessity of a colossal Kulturkampf, to make science a religion, or of creating a vast intellectual organization—the biggest ever—to propagate it.

At this crucial point Mr. Wells strikes us as pedantically dogmatic. He says that the adaptation which is needed to arrest the present drive towards disaster is the re-education of man as a conscious world-citizen. With that we entirely agree. He goes on to say: "The scientific vision of the universe and no other (*sic*) has to be his vision of the universe." This is surely a palpable *non sequitur*. What *is* the scientific vision of the universe? Which of the innumerable perspectives of science is to be authoritative? Why not that which assures us that at some future time this planet will be incapable of supporting life? Or that which tells us that our mundane affairs are an infinitesimal fraction of the goings-on of the stellar universe? The re-education of men in the conviction that they are citizens of the world needs a basis more solid and more human than this. And it is difficult to understand why Mr. Wells so passionately rejects as a possible basis for his world citizenship the Christian notion of the brotherhood of men. He may have convinced himself that it has been tried, and failed. But, if that were true, what greater hope is there of establishing the kind of sublime technocracy which is his dream. Why should we trust the men of science? Mr. Wells himself finds the dogmatic Marxism of Mr. J. B. S. Haldane and Mr. Bernal intolerably narrow. Other people find the scientism of Mr. Wells himself distinctly blinkered. Ecology may be very well to help us to understand our desperate situation; it has singularly little to tell us on how we may escape the worst. When we come

down from the heights of the big biological generalization to the level on which the first steps have to be taken,
Mr. Wells has no guidance to give. Create a super-university, compose a world-encyclopaedia! These are not
solutions, but evasions of the problem—flattering, no
doubt to the prospective professors and contributors,
but, even if they were practicable, quite without power
to capture the hearts and inspire the wills of youths and
men.

It is singular and instructive that Mr. Wells never
faces his own problem on the truly human level. On that
level it is a new form of the old problem of overcoming
the natural egotism of men, whether as individuals or
small or large societies. Even knowledge is sought by the
great majority of men for their own aggrandisement,
whether crudely material or more subtly social. Beneath
the deceptive phrase "creating an adequate mental organization" is hidden the more exacting and more
familiar requirement of a moral regeneration of mankind.

At no point does Mr. Wells show himself really aware
of what is actually involved in the adaptation of *Homo
sapiens* to his new conditions. He is bemused by his own
scientific terminology, and succumbs to the superficial
notion that it is truly comprehensive. "The scientific
vision and no other": so runs the new Athanasian creed.
Therefore, instead of pointing the need of a new kind of
regenerated men, he is satisfied that a new association
of "superior persons" will suffice. It is true he despairs of
getting it. Perhaps it is as well. For, if the salvation of
the world did really depend on a new encyclopaedia, the
simple man could contribute nothing towards it. The
wisdom the world needs to-day is one which humbles the
wise no less than the simple. Mr. Wells is impressed by
the achievement of the "Encyclopédie"; perhaps if he
were to study its history again he would discover that it
became dynamic through the most recalcitrant of its
members—the one who walked out of a dinner party of
his colleagues with the words: "Et moi, messieurs, je
crois en Dieu!"

15

T. S. Eliot's *The Idea of a Christian Society*

Only those who have done some hard thinking for themselves concerning the nature and destiny of contemporary society will appreciate how much objective analysis and self-scrutiny has gone to the making of this slim book by Mr. T. S. Eliot on "the Idea of a Christian Society." It was written before the outbreak of war; its origination, Mr. Eliot tells us, was in the moral shock produced upon him by the crisis of September, 1938, which caused in him "a feeling of humiliation . . . not a criticism of the government but a doubt of the validity of a civilization." But it was written with the possibility of war in mind, and it is acutely pertinent to the situation to-day.

What is the idea—in Coleridge's sense of the word—of the society in which we live? Mr. Eliot begins by asking. We conceive of it under several different phrases the meaning of which we forbear to examine; they are regarded as sacrosanct, as sufficient in themselves to establish the superiority of our form of society over its new and now insistent rivals. We speak of it sometimes as a "liberal" society, less often as a "Christian" society; but the blessed word which is chiefly used to validate it is "democracy." Of our claim to be a Christian society Mr. Eliot quickly disposes:

The Idea of a Christian Society. By T. S. Eliot. Faber and Faber. (*Times Literary Supplement*, 4 November 1939.)

To speak of ourselves as a Christian society in contrast to that of Germany or Russia, is an abuse of terms. We mean only that we have a society in which no one is penalized for the *formal profession* of Christianity; but we conceal from ourselves the unpleasant knowledge of the real values by which we live.

At this point we must break into Mr. Eliot's argument, in order to interpose that we mean a little more than this, if and when we call ourselves a Christian society. We may be mistaken in our belief, but we do believe that there is something Christian in the principle of political equality; that it is an expression in the political realm of the respect for human personality which Christianity inculcates. This expression may be inappropriate or exaggerated or premature; and certainly it is preposterous to call ourselves a Christian society on the strength of it: but just as certainly it is a part of what is intended when we apply that adjective to ourselves.

Mr. Eliot, however, declares that he does not understand what is meant by democracy, as the word is used to-day; and he is on firm ground when he insists that the word "does not contain enough positive content to stand alone against forces you dislike—it can easily be transformed by them," for what is in fact meant by "democracy" is a system that might well be used to introduce totalitarianism. In so far as the word includes the attitudes known as "liberalism," it is enough to say that they are disappearing; the sphere of private life which "liberalism" nominally defends is being steadily whittled away. The tradition of "liberalism" derives from our achievement and successful practice of religious toleration; but that worked because in fact the members of the various communions were all substantially agreed in their assumptions concerning social morality. The comfortable distinction between public and private morality is no longer valid; now the individual is increasingly implicated in a network of social and economic institutions from which, even when he is aware of their control of his behaviour, he cannot extricate himself. The operation of these institutions is no longer neutral, but non-Christian. Mr. Eliot sums up his examination of the present condition of our society: It is in a neutral or negative condition; it has ceased in any effective sense to be a Christian society; and, if the forces now operative are allowed to continue without a deliberate and success-ful attempt to control them towards specifically Chris-tian ends—an effort of which the magnitude can only be dimly conceived—this neutral condition of society will either proceed to a gradual decline "or (whether as the result of catastrophe or not) reform itself into a positive shape which is likely to be effectively secular."

Unfortunately, the majority of people who think about contemporary society regard the second alternative as the ideal, and even a majority of the professed Chris-tians who think about it are content with it. As Mr. Eliot dryly observes, we need not assume that this secular society will be very like any at present observable: "The Anglo-Saxons display a capacity for *diluting* their reli-gion, probably in excess of that of any other race." But those to whom a diluted religion of the state is as repug-nant as the prospect of what D. H. Lawrence called "the greasy slipping into decay" should make up their minds that the only possibility left is that of a positive Chris-tian society, the idea of which Mr. Eliot proceeds to outline.

He distinguishes three elements, or aspects, of the Christian society: the Christian state, the Christian com-munity, and the community of Christians. First, the men of state, who need not be ardent Christians, must at least have been educated to think in Christian catego-ries, and be confined both by their own habit of mind and the temper and tradition of the people to a Chris-tian "frame of reference." Second comes the Christian community, whose Christianity will be largely uncon-scious, and consist mainly in religious observances and traditions of behaviour: "The mass of the population in a Christian society should not be exposed to a way of life in which there is too sharp and frequent a conflict between what their circumstances dictate and what is Christian." This condition is very far from being fulfilled in England to-day; the life of the remoter rural parish comes nearest to it, but this has not been typical of English life for a century, and is, even now, still in rapid decline. Modern industrialism has produced a world to which traditional Christian social forms are ill adapted. The notion of adapting Christian social ideals to the forms of life imposed by industrialism is a false simplification, whereby Christianity resigns all claims to shape society. So is the idea of returning, by an act of the moral will, to a simpler mode of life: if that happens, it will be from natural causes.

> Few will dispute that a great deal of the machinery of modern life is merely a sanction for non-Christian aims, that it is not only hostile to the conscious pursuit of the Christian life in the world by the few, but to the maintenance of any Christian society *of* the world. We must abandon the notion that the Christian should be content with freedom of cultus, and with suffering no worldly disabilities on account of his faith. However bigoted the announcement may sound, the Christian can be satisfied with nothing less than a Christian organization of society—which is not the same thing as a society consisting exclusively of devout Christians. It would be a society in which the natural end of man—virtue and well-being in community—is acknowledged for all, and the supernatural end, beatitude, for those who have eyes to see it.

To prevent the tendency of the State towards expedience and cynicism, and of the mass of the people towards lethargy and superstition is the function of the third element—the "community of Christians," composed of both clergy and laity of superior intellectual or spiritual gifts, which would give the tone to the educational systems, consolidate a religious basis for the culture of society and "collectively form the conscious mind and conscience of the nation."

The Christian society, thus outlined, is one to which the Church could be in vital relation: by its hierarchy in direct and official relation to the State, by its parochial system in contact with the smallest units and individual members of the community and in the persons of its more eminent "clerks" forming part of the community of Christians. A national Church is therefore necessary —a Church which aims at comprehending the whole nation; but the idea of the national Church must be counterpoised by the idea of the universal Church. Only if it fully recognizes its position as part of the universal Church can the national Church combat the tendency to religious-social integration on the lower level of State or race. The prior loyalty of the member of the national Church is to the universal Church.

> It must be kept in mind that even in a Christian society as well organized as we can conceive possible in this world, the limit would be that our temporal and spiritual life should be harmonized: the temporal and spiritual world would never be identified. There would always remain a dual allegiance to the State and to the Church, to one's countrymen and to one's fellow-Christians everywhere, and the latter would always have the primacy. There would always be a tension: and this tension is essential to the idea of a Christian society and is a distinguishing mark between a Christian and a pagan society.

It is inherent in the nature of Mr. Eliot's argument that he does not entertain the illusion that it would be easy to bring such a society into being. Not only are the social, economic and political processes actually in motion to-day carrying society away from, not towards, such a goal, but to the majority of the *intelligentsia* the goal itself is undesirable. First, because such an idea of the good society is Christian in a definite sense which is alien to the ordinary vague use of the word and perhaps intolerable to the "liberal" mind; secondly, because such an organization of society (though it is quite reconcilable with our English political system) is, in the true sense of the word, aristocratic. That is enough to scare the "democrat," who is seldom realistic enough to analyze the structure of the democratic society in which we live, or to form a clear conception of the nature of the controlling powers in it.

If such a critical attitude towards our society were more prevalent, so would be a realization of the new urgency of the perennial problem of politics: how is power to be made responsible? *Quis custodiet ipsos custodes?* The events of the last twenty years should have compelled us to ponder that problem more anxiously than we are naturally inclined to do: for our instinct, confirmed by a century of relatively privileged and prosperous living, is to trust to the general "sense of decency" in the depositories of power, and to the efficacy of popular protest against abuses of power. A "sense of decency" requires a smiling climate to make it reliable; and under the new strain of totalitarian war, which presses hardest on the professional classes among whom the "sense of decency" is chiefly cherished, it may collapse with surprising rapidity.

Yet the task of strengthening this ethos, or rather of regenerating it—for nothing less is in question—is being practically disregarded. We seem unable to recognize the relevance to ourselves of the new totalitarian systems. The relevance is great and alarming: for by our political tradition we are accustomed finally to rely on popular protest as the remedy for abuse of power; but the startling success of the new techniques of Government and propaganda should have taught us that the very impulse to popular protest can be stifled with ease. The true nature of the problem of the responsibility of power is revealed: it is not, as it seemed to be, a problem of checks and balances but one of religion, ethics and education. The constantly accelerating movement towards social integration on the material level puts decisive power more and more into politically irresponsible hands. The theory of responsibility to Parliament and to the people remains; but the theory corresponds less and less to the sociological reality.

Hence the incessant cry for coordination—another of the blessed words by which we are bemused. For at best this would be a coordination of mechanisms, sufficient supervision to ensure that the cogs do not revolve in different directions and strip one another. Subordination is more nearly what is required; a widespread acknowledgment of the ends for which society exists, and a common recognition of a hierarchy of values by which its activities can be ordered—in short, a system of spiritual and ethical priorities to which, even in time of war, the system of mechanical and productive priorities must be subordinated, or with which it must at least be harmonized.

Such a system can only be based on religious postulates. The totalitarian regimes have these religious postulates. Because they happen to be repugnant to us we have no right to deny that they exist; or that, though at a low level, they are explicit and coherent. What have we to oppose to them? We have a sentimental respect for the individual, which, because it is sentimental, offers no resistance to economic and social processes which steadily diminish the concrete reality of the individual—the person exercising responsible freedom. We have a fairly rich array of vestigial Christian values compacted together in the form of a tradition of political and personal freedom which is more a legend than a reality. Probably Mr. Eliot is right when he says that what we chiefly dislike about totalitarianism is the element of authority; being scared of overt and responsible authority we submit, unwittingly, to the constant encroachments of clandestine and irresponsible authority.

As Mr. Eliot recognizes, there is no short way out of the condition in which we are. If we are to avoid, or to even have the power of overcoming, secular totalitarianism, we have to begin at the beginning. The work to hand is primarily a work of education both in the more specific and the more general sense. The latter comes first. Of the elements of the Christian society the first we can hope to bring partly into being is "the community of Christians," a body of people persuaded that the Christian conception of man is the necessary foundation of a politics that can contend against the demonic forces of a machine age. There, no doubt, is a prime difficulty. Christianity in England, when it is not a social convention, tends to be individualistic, emotional and eccentric; that it is a system of truth from which flow inexhaustible governing principles in metaphysics, ethics and politics is too rarely admitted even as a possibility by the intelligent man. To bring the contemporary intelligence to an attitude of respect for Christian thought is an undertaking as arduous as it is urgent. Mr. Eliot's book is a very valuable contribution towards this end.

16

C. G. Jung's *Psychological Types*

The struggle between Freud and Jung is by now vaguely familiar to the educated world. It knows that the erstwhile colleagues have parted, as Nietzsche and Wagner parted many years ago; perhaps it has an inkling of why they parted. If it cares to know the substantial truth of the whole story, it will find it, by implication, throughout this lengthy book.

And it ought to care. Whatever may be the value finally set on Freud and Jung in themselves, their conflict has a very real symbolical significance. To understand it is to understand, from a new angle, the *impasse* of the modern consciousness and to gain a fresh vision of the problem which in one disguise or another confronts the man who is aware of himself and his age.

Freud and Jung began their work with the investigation of neuroses, maladies of the being which doubtless have existed for centuries, but which, if only for the frequency with which they are recognized, may rightly be called characteristically modern. People went melancholy mad, of course, long before neuroses were heard of. Many of the English poets of the eighteenth century —to take a single striking case—were either actually clapped in madhouses or on the brink of it. They were the extreme cases; the more moderate knew what they

Psychological Types; or The Psychology of Individuation. By C. G. Jung. Translated with an Introduction by H. G. Baynes. Kegan Paul. (*Nation and Athenaeum,* 17 March 1923.)

had to expect in those substantial times, and kept their disabilities to themselves. Nevertheless, the neurosis is a modern malady. Under a different name, and less openly, it affected the eighteenth no less than the nineteenth century. But the eighteenth century also is modern. So is the seventeenth, at the beginning of which we clearly see John Ford, "deep in dump with a melancholy hat." And heaven alone knows what John Webster looked like. Prince Hamlet was surely nothing compared to him.

Neuroses—to risk a great generalization which may not be so fantastic as it appears—belong to the world that followed the Renaissance, the modern world in the largest and most significant sense of the term. From the moment the individual began to assert himself against the theocratic scheme of things, neuroses lay in wait for him. Not so much because the more enlightened spirits began to bear the burden of their individual destinies alone—though this isolation of the individual counted for much—as because in the old scheme of things there was a place for neuroses. The medieval neurotic may have been abnormal, but he was legitimate. The broad bosom of the universal Church had room for him. The nervous affliction of the body was the mark of the finger of God; the neurotic in mind was a visionary, a seer, a chosen servant of the Divine.

But since that time, since the day when the Renaissance broke the dam of the great reservoir and left Western humanity to flood out and find its own level, the neurotics had no home. In the eighteenth century they were isolated and persecuted; though practically the whole of the literary achievement of the century was their work. In the nineteenth they began to organize themselves. For their own protection they invented the conception of "Art." In other words, they made a religion for themselves, having learnt at last that the threadbare caricature of the old religion had no room for them; it had no room for them because it had degenerated into a mere projection of the average man's desire to insure himself against discomfort from his conscience now and the possibility of discomfort from the hands of God hereafter.

Of course, not all neurotics were artists. But the artist is the neurotic who impresses himself on the memory of mankind; and he may fairly be regarded as the memorable type of his great kind. But why verge on the Nordau-esque and call him neurotic? Simply because he is. Neurosis is maladjustment to the social demand. The artist is that neurotic who has the fortunate privilege of being able to satisfy his maladjustment by an unpractical and ideal creation; the rest of them are not so lucky. But is there not a social demand for the work of the artist? There is also a social demand for *cul-de-jattes*, sword-swallowers, one-eyed men who will put their heads in tigers' mouths, and other curiosities. Humanity gets sick of its own deadly average, and sometimes needs something other than the biggest thing on earth to gape at. It, too, has a thwarted craving for the mysterious and uncircumscribed; it loves to be safe, but it likes to fear; it glues its nose to the grindstone, but it still dreams dreams. Some of its dreams are high and noble, some of its discontents divine. It gets the artist to appease them. But not even in the rare case when it conceives an admiration for him does it wish to be as he. He is a freak who comes in handy, like the white-eyed kaffir.

"Adjust or be damned" is the unspoken sentiment of the modern world. And simply because the compulsion is become so tremendous, gathering force as it goes, the cries of the maladjusted, who have no Art to work their freedom in or religion to give them rest, begin to echo and re-echo through modern society. And Freud and Jung, who went to the work as doctors, in attacking neuroses, attacked a central point. They did not know what they were up against. One thinks of them as a couple of decent men who smelt a strange smell. One of them went along with a box of matches; the other with an electric torch. And there, issuing out of a very small manhole, was the sizzle and smell of a most unpleasant gas. The man with the matches prized up the lid. Then he struck a match. He was blown into kingdom come. That was Herr Doktor Freud. Herr Doktor Jung, with the torch, has emerged into daylight with a very green face to tell the trembling story.

Herr Doktor Freud's last audible word was "Sex"; Herr Doktor Jung stammers "Lib-libido." But what "Lib-libido" is, Herr Doktor Jung is frightened to say. He has a queer notion that it is—well, everything. Life itself, the *primum mobile.*

And the real question is: What is to be done about it? The gas is escaping still. That small explosion was merely anticipatory, as it were a parlor demonstration of its high inflammability. A more satisfactory one to this generation avid of biggest things on earth was the Crystal Palace display of the War. A twittering ghost of Herr Doktor Freud experiments with unlucky patients and changes their neuroses into much more uncomfortable ones. Herr Doktor Jung murmurs that he must make the individual an individual. Each neurotic, he whispers, is unique, and contains the potentialities of a unique being. He is unique already, Herr Doktor; the question is: How can he become a being? And the Herr Doktor rolls a vague and pansynoptic eye over the history of the human spirit, waves a feeble hand towards the East, repeats his special abracadabra "Extrointroextrointrovertebrate" eleven times, and subsides into his professional chair. Six-hundred-and-forty mortal pages to tell us that it's all wrong, and not a word of how to put it right. One wonders with what he keep himself going.

Poor Herr Doktor! It is a tragedy. Not the less for being ours as well as yours. You are an able man; and it must be a grim sort of joke for you to have your English translator enthusiastically expounding the triumphant merit of your "crowning work," when you know it is your declaration of bankruptcy. But you should have read Dostoevsky, you know, instead of wasting your time, patriotically but absurdly, on Herr Spitteler, who was given the Nobel Prize in preference to Thomas Hardy. If you had read "The Brothers Karamazov" you need not have wasted all these years. You would have found your old Libido in the Father, its modern perversions in Ivan and Dmitri and Smerdiakov, and the miracle in Alyosha. You could have spent these years in thinking how the miracle might be produced, instead of ending them with a bewildered realization that a miracle is necessary and that you are not Almighty God to perform it. It was a pity you stopped at Nietzsche.

Under the great tome "Psychological Types" Jung has buried psycho-analysis. It is an adequate tombstone. Nothing will be able to lift it. Even I am competent to carve the epitaph upon it: "Here lies Psycho-Analysis, which may have helped a few to be conscious of their problem, but which helped nobody to solve it."

But it is a little ironical that the neurotics should know so much more than their doctors.

17

Sigmund Freud's *Moses and Monotheism*

"Moses and Monotheism"—the work of one of the great original thinkers of our time—bears in its substance the impress of the strange period in which it was composed. As Dr. Freud explains, in an interlude the more impressive for its reticence, the book is composed of three parts, two of which were published in the Viennese psycho-analytical periodical *Imago*; but the third was deliberately withheld in order to avoid giving offence to the Catholic authorities of Austria, who tolerated the continuance of psycho-analytical practice and teaching, but (the author feared) might have ceased to do so if he had published the third part of the book, in which the Jewish and the Christian religions—though given their traditional pre-eminence in the spiritual history of Europe—are explained on the analogy of the Freudian interpretation of neurosis. The National-Socialist invasion put an end at once to the toleration and the need for compromise; compelled to take refuge in England, Freud was free to finish his book, but he felt himself unable to remove the traces of its interrupted composition. He apologizes for the repetitions it contains. They offend his sense of form. Nevertheless, in the case of a writer who practises such severe economy of statement and whose interpretation of the history of religion is so revolutionary, the three-fold recapitulation of his theme is by no means

Moses and Monotheism. By Sigmund Freud. Translated by Katherine Jones. Hogarth Press. (*Times Literary Supplement*, 27 May 1939.)

excessive. Moreover, his book contains the meditations of one of the most distinguished of living Jews on the destiny and significance of his race at a crucial moment in its history.

The book is impressive. In a sense it is beyond criticism. Thus, it is really immaterial whether or not we accept the novel hypothesis with which it begins—namely, that Moses was an Egyptian. It is a matter on which certainty is unattainable. That the traditional Hebrew derivation of the name Moses is untenable, and that it is probably an Egyptian word, meaning "child" or "son," has for some time been generally admitted. We can honourably accord "the willing suspension of disbelief" to the suggestion that Moses was actually an Egyptian of rank who was a convinced adherent of the monotheism promulgated by Ikhnaton. In the period of polytheistic reaction and political anarchy which followed Ikhnaton's death (the story continues) Moses, in order that monotheism might not perish, made himself the leader of the denizen Israelites, imposed his religion —and above all the practice of circumcision—upon them, and led them out of Egypt. Subsequently, the Israelites rebelled and reverted to a Canaanitish Baal-worship; and—for this novel detail Freud invokes the evidence of Sellin—killed Moses. But his immediate followers, like himself of Egyptian origin, retained their allegiance to monotheism. At Kadesh—here Eduard Meyer becomes the authority—a new religion, of the volcano-god Jahve, was accepted by the Israelites who had now joined with other tribes; and a kind of religious compromise effected between the priest of Jahve—a second "Moses" of nomad Midianite origin, and the "Levite" followers of the original Egyptian Moses. Circumcision was accepted as the distinctive rite of the Jahve religion, and the original Moses acknowledged as the father of the people; thus Jahve became the god of the Exodus.

The Exodus and the founding of the new religion were thus brought together in time, the long interval between them being denied. The bestowal of the Ten Commandments too was said to have taken place not at Kadesh, but at the foot of the Holy Mountain amidst the signs of a volcanic eruption. This description, however, did a serious wrong to the memory of the man Moses; it was he, and not the volcano-god, who had freed his people from Egypt. Some compensation was therefore due to him, and it was given by transposing Moses to Kadesh or to the mount Sinai-Horeb, and putting him in the place of the Midianite priest.

In course of time the temporarily submerged monotheistic tradition emerged again, and was constantly reinforced by the prophets, until finally it became completely triumphant.

That is a summary account of the first, historical, section of the book. It is revolutionary; but those who fully admit all the implications of Old Testament criticism will allow that the field is at least free for such a hypothesis, and that the hypothesis itself is a bold and broad attempt to account for the origination of Jewish monotheism, and for the profound dualism that runs through the Hexateuch. The connexion of Jewish monotheism with the monotheism of Ikhnaton is difficult to avoid, if the historicity of the captivity in Egypt be accepted. The difficulty for the ordinary person nourished, however unconsciously, in the Christian tradition is to entertain the notion that monotheism needs to be accounted for at all. Freud has no doubt that the rise of monotheism needs explanation; and he believes that its origination in Egypt can be explained by the political conditions there. Under Thothmes III Egypt had become a world power, comprising Nubia, Palestine, Syria and part of Mesopotamia. "This imperialism was reflected in religion as Universality and Monotheism." A marked peculiarity of Ikhnaton's monotheism was its complete rejection of the belief in immortality and the after-life. The same peculiarity attached to Mosaic monotheism. But whereas in the case of Egypt the peculiarity is explicable, because Ikhnaton's religious movement was developed in opposition to the popular religion which was concentrated on the after-life, in the case of the Mosaic religion it is inexplicable. This, and adoption of circumcision "to remove the reproach of Egypt"—to use the significant phrase from the book of Joshua—together with the Egyptian origin of the name of Moses, make a strong case for Freud's hypothesis.

But this is merely introductory to the problem with which he is concerned. How is it, he asks, that monotheism, once originated, takes so deep root in the mind of man, so that it appears to men as though in discovering monotheism they had laid hold of an eternal truth hitherto concealed from them? The answer of the religious mind is that it appears to men as eternal because it *is* eternal truth.

> I also should like to accept this solution. However, I have my misgivings. The religious argument is based on an optimistic and idealistic premise. The human intellect has not shown itself elsewhere to be endowed with a very good scent for truth, nor has the human mind displayed any special readiness to accept truth.

Monotheism comes to the human mind with the compulsiveness of religious truth, says Freud, because it comes enforced with the reanimated memory of a tremendous primeval experience, which must have been crucial in the pre-history of the human race. The theory which Freud here develops was originally put forward by him in 1912, in "Totem and Taboo." Taking from Darwin the hypothesis that men originally lived in small hordes under the rule of an older male who governed by brute force; from Atkinson the suggestion that this system came to an end through a concerted rebellion of the sons, who killed and consumed the father; and from Robertson Smith the notion that this primeval patriarchy was succeeded by a totem brother-clan in which exogamy was practised, he reconstructed a primitive prehistorical drama, universal in the experience of mankind, analogous to that which he had discovered in the psychical history of the individual. The pre-historical slaying of the father—at once venerated and dreaded, a source of strength and weakness to the sons—occupies in the evolution of the human race as a whole the same position as the repressed experiences—the parent-complexes—of childhood have in the development of the person.

This hypothesis serves to explain the clinically observed peculiarity whereby reactions to traumata in the individual are frequently not confined to the field of the individual's own experience; on the strength of this clinical observation Freud maintains that "the archaic heritage of mankind does not include only dispositions, but ideational contacts, memory-traces of the experiences of former generations," but he does not admit the necessity of Jung's further hypothesis of "the collective unconscious."

It is necessary to stress the fact that Freud was compelled to problems of pre-history or psychological anthropology by his own clinical investigations into problems of psychopathology; unless this is appreciated it may be thought that his treatment of ethnological material is arbitrary, in particular his refusal to allow that the anthropological hypotheses which he adopted in 1912 have been superseded by later theories. "Above all," he says pertinently, "I am not an ethnologist, but a psycho-analyst. It was my good right to select from ethnological data what would serve me for my analytic work." Perhaps the modesty is misplaced which prevents him from asserting that, in his view, the congruity of anthropological theory with his psychological investigations is a criterion of its validity. The claim remains implicit; but it is inevitable. Psycho-analysis does offer a clue to human pre-history, and it is lack of imagination which persuades many anthropologists that Freud's investigations are irrelevant to their science, and his judgments upon it without weight.

The large-scale problem which Freud seeks to solve in the history of the Jewish people is that of the re-emergence and gradual triumph of Mosaic monotheism after the adoption of Jahve—a fierce, tribal god—by the Israelites: why it was that "in the course of time Jahve lost his own character and became more and more like the old god of Moses, Aton." Freud puts aside the idea of a spontaneous development towards a higher spirituality, because "it does not explain anything." Moreover, the political condition of the Jews was definitely inimical to a movement away from the idea of an exclusive national God towards that of a universal God. In brief, Freud's solution is this. The universal tendency towards monotheism, which derives from the slaying of the primeval father of the horde, in the case of the Jews was powerfully reinforced by the slaying of Moses—their great monotheistic leader. The primeval drama was re-enacted at the level of consciousness, and the compulsiveness of the idea of the father-God made infinitely more potent. The combination of the peculiar compulsiveness of the idea, and the luckless history of the Jewish people, made inevitable a simultaneous exaltation of monotheism and a deepening sense of guilt—which was refined under the influence of the prophets into an inextricable association between sanctity and suffering, between being the chosen people and being oppressed. Yet a third time the Jews slew their leader in the person of Christ; and another great Jew, Paul, by an act of profound insight seized upon the feeling of guilt and "correctly traced it back to its primeval source."

> This he called original sin; it was a crime against God that could be expiated only by death. In reality, this crime, deserving of death, had been the murder of the Father who later was deified. The murderous deed itself, however, was not remembered; in its place stood the phantasy of expiation and that is why this phantasy could be welcomed in the form of a gospel of salvation. A Son of God, innocent himself, had sacrificed himself—and had thereby taken over the guilt of the world. It had to be a Son, for the sin had been murder of the Father.

Thus Paul—"a man with a gift for religion in the truest sense of the phrase"—by developing the Jewish religion to its extreme point, destroyed it, first, by laying the ghost of the feeling of guilt, and then by giving up the idea of the chosen people and its visible sign, circumcision. In some respects the new religion was a retrogression; it surrendered much of the strictness of its monotheism, abated some of its spirituality, made room for the mother-goddess and found subordinate niches for many other polytheistic deities. It was in part a renewed triumph of the priests of Ammon over the god of Ikhnaton. Nevertheless, it marked a progress in the history of religion. Whereas the Jewish religion would not admit the murder of the father-God, Christianity did virtually admit it and was purified. But anti-Semitism does not derive from this superiority; it is the reaction of recent and "badly Christened" Christians, who have not overcome their grudge against the religion that was forced upon them. "Hatred for Judaism is at bottom hatred for Christianity."

One cannot avoid doing violence to Freud's argument by such a summary. Whatever be one's opinion of its separate elements, one must acknowledge that it bears the marks of genius. It is a transparent book, and it is a deep one. Of it, even more truly than of "Totem and Taboo," in which the words occur, it may be said that "it makes possible a deeper understanding and offers a hypothesis which may seem fantastic but which has the advantage of establishing an unexpected unity among a series of hitherto separated phenomena."

18

Ernest Seillière's *Alexandre Vinet: Historien de la Pensée Française*

It is curious that the work of M. Ernest Seillière, who is the *doyen* of philosophical critics of romanticism, should be less known in England than that of his followers, Mr. Irving Babbitt in America and M. Pierre Lasserre in France. Both these authors are under a heavy debt to M. Seillière, who has been occupied for the best part of a life-time in writing a critical history of romanticism in all its French and some of its German and Russian and English manifestations. Hardly a year passes without his adding at least one substantial chapter to his work, in the form of a special study of some particular figure in the romantic succession.

The romantic succession is prodigiously long, for romanticism is one of the perennial modes of the human spirit. No matter where, or at what time, we investigate the records of the spiritual activity of mankind, there we find indubitable traces of the secular antithesis between the individual and the institution, between tradition and revelation; it appears to be the essential movement of intellectual and spiritual life. Romanticism after romanticism is organized into classicism after classicism, only for each classicism to be first disrupted and then revivified by a subsequent romanticism. And it seems that the results of most permanent value are those which are

Alexandre Vinet: Historien de la Pensée Française. Suivi d'un appendice sur Henri-Frédéric Amiel. Par Ernest Seillière. Paris: Payot. (*Times Literary Supplement*, 29 July 1926.)

achieved by a concentration of the antinomy and a solution of it in the mind of a single man. Of no one of the truly outstanding figures in the history of humanity whose words or whose works remain incessantly fruitful in contact with the understanding mind can it be said simply: "This man was a romantic," or: "This man was a classic." The pure romantics and the pure classics are all forgotten, for the pure romantic is unintelligible and the pure classicist not worth the trouble of understanding.

This radical conception of the life-giving antinomy between romanticism and classicism, the habit of considering them as secular modes of the human spirit, is not very familiar in England, for the sufficient reason that our institutions early in our history acquired an elasticity which is the envy and the despair of the foreigner. Magna Charta and Habeas Corpus have been potent prophylactics against the erection of that absolute authority which sooner or later compels absolute rebellion. By cutting off one king's head we insured ourselves against the necessity of a hecatomb. The extraordinary difference between the Church of England and the various forms of Continental Protestantism, the curious sense of emotional barrenness with which a temple of the Reformed Church in France or Switzerland afflicts the ordinary Englishman, is striking evidence of our instinctive skill as a nation in choosing a middle way. Nor can it fairly be put down to insular egotism that we feel a pride in our native methods; for, after all, we scarcely know what it is that we feel proud about, and if we did we should have lost the cause for pride. Therefore we choose apparently irrelevant symbols for our quiet feeling of self-gratulation—meandering English hedges, for example, move us profoundly after a few days travelling over the ordered Continent. There is, in truth, a world of significance in an English hedge. It is the *via media* between a wall and a paling fence. As against the wall it signifies a lack of haste in asserting one's rights; as against the paling fence, that these rights will not

quickly be challenged, and in itself an instinctive conviction that the best things are the things which grow. A
country of hedges can be neither romantic nor classic.
That is probably why in England these epithets are
either neglected altogether as irrelevant, or bandied
about with an astonishing *insouciance*. Romanticism, for
most English readers, is just something that happened to
English poetry at the beginning of the nineteenth century. If they go a step farther and ask why it was that
most of those romantic poets regarded themselves not as
innovators but as restorers of the Elizabethan tradition,
they are confronted with the problem why the Elizabethans themselves are not called romantics. The most
frequent answer to the problem is that they were Elizabethans. So romanticism once more becomes a quality
peculiar to a handful of English poets at the beginning
of the nineteenth century—a quality vaguely compounded of lyricism and a capacity for ecstatic feeling in
the presence of nature. Since the Elizabethans were no
mean lyricists, the residuum seems to be nature-worship.

That description of romanticism would be pregnant
enough were it not for the English habit of using the
term "nature" almost exclusively of inanimate nature.
The romanticism that is not, so to speak, a mere episode
in the autobiography of English literature, but a secular
and omnipresent tendency of the human mind, is the
worship of nature in a larger sense than this. The individual who breaks away, in thought or word or act, from
the laws, customs and conventions of the society in
which he lives, claiming the right to think or speak or act
as seems good to himself, is a romantic. What seems
good to him may be better and truer than what is approved by laws, customs and conventions; it may be
worse and less true. If he conceives of nature as a mere
absence of law, the thoughts and acts of the romantic
who follows nature will be less good, for law is a necessity of spiritual life; if nature is conceived as itself a
law-giver, giving laws of a subtler and more exacting kind
than can be conveyed and formulated in ordinances and

conventions, then the thoughts and words and acts of the romantic will be better and truer than those of the society in which he lives. These two conceptions, of nature as a condition of licence and of nature as the source of a higher law, are both included in romanticism. Not infrequently they are present in the same person. It is impossible, for instance, to understand Rousseau, except by seeing him as wavering incessantly, and almost unconsciously, between the two attitudes. How difficult they are to distinguish clearly appears in the peculiarly Christian manifestation of the romantic experience, the scruple of conscience. Conscience, or the inner voice, is generally regarded as promulgating a higher law than that of the State, or even the Church, and has even reached the paradoxical position of being allowed for by the law itself: yet a good many objections are let pass as conscientious which are almost certainly libertarian. But it is beyond human power to distinguish between true conscience and the sham one save by their works. So, indeed, with the whole problem of romanticism in its most general sense: the words of Gamaliel concerning the new superstition that had sprung up in Jerusalem are the words of wisdom. Time alone will show whether it is true.

The relation between romanticism and Christianity, with which M. Seillière has especially concerned himself, is singularly interesting. For the philosophical critic must regard the founder of the Christian religion as an almost pure case of the romantic, whose own individual and separate experience of God was certain and strong enough to carry him to the supreme act of self-sacrifice on behalf of humanity. As a teacher he declared the higher law of nature: to regain the innocence of the child was the condition of man's entering the Kingdom of God. But such an experience and such a faith, though they have been the inspiration of all man's sublimest spiritual achievements since, were too sublime for the ruck of men. To be made viable, the romanticism needed to be organized into a classicism, and the great classical Christian doctrine of original sin was framed. So long as this doctrine remains fundamental to Christian psychology, Christianity may be said to be substantially anti-romantic; but when it is pressed to an extreme it becomes so false to human experience and so oppressive to human nature that a compensating romanticism is necessary. This happened with the Reformers, who were compelled to mitigate the effects of their doctrine of original sin by a highly mystical and miraculous conception of grace; moreover, as M. Seillière points out, it is true in a sense that the doctrine of predestination is allied to the romantic notion of "natural salvation." It was perhaps to be expected that the great romantic of modern times should have been born in the small country where the doctrine of original sin was pushed to its extremest conclusions. Rousseau is, after all, a singularly un-French writer, and probably the extravagance of his genius is best explained by the vehemence of his reaction against the utterly pessimistic psychology of Geneva. The pendulum swung, as it were, from a false classicism to a false romanticism. In Vinet and Amiel M. Seillière studies two later representatives of the Swiss mind, in whom the fundamental Puritanism of the race—there is not a little Puritanism in Jean-Jacques—is tempered by æsthetic sensibility to a pale and beautiful austerity. M. Seillière has done well to bring Vinet and Amiel together, for the kinship between the two men was profound, the chief difference being that Amiel belongs to a generation after Vinet. His scepticism has dissolved away the fundamentals of Christian belief to which Vinet so loyally held. Amiel himself was well aware of the relation between them. In November, 1852, he wrote in his Journal:

> Je n'ai jamais senti comme aujourd'hui ma parenté d'esprit avec Vinet, le psychologue moraliste, le critique devin et juge. Je crois que je pourrais le *continuer*, car ma plus visible aptitude est de même nature et peut-être pas de moindre degré. Il me semble même avoir des ressources, une étendue, un horizon peut-être plus grands . . . Comme chrétien, je lui serai toujours inférieur:

comme penseur je serais heureux d'arriver à être son égal:
comme écrivain je puis espérer peut-être davantage.

That was a just and prophetic estimate. Amiel is the
greater writer, the lesser Christian. But Vinet and he are
of the same type. We may fairly call it the finest Protestant type. Both were convinced of the supremacy of
conscience; both had an instinctive aptitude for the
beauty of morality. They were both representatives,
within the limits of a distinctively Protestant tradition,
of that harmonious combination of the romantic and
classical impulses of which we have spoken. Both were
individualists; both sought from their individualism the
opportunity of a finer discipline than was offered by any
institutions; both were lonely men. In another century
they might both have found a spiritual home in Port-
Royal.

M. Seillière presents them both as accomplished types
of Christian romanticism, Vinet still within the Church,
Amiel having passed outside it. As a literary critic Vinet
is sensibly Amiel's inferior, for his criticism of the unbri-
dled romanticism of nineteenth-century France, though
penetrating, is too heavily weighted with the moral pre-
conception: his æsthetic admirations and his moral
judgments are not harmonized, so that he too often
appears to be giving back with the right hand what he
has taken away with the left. As a critical historian of
Christianity he is, however, of the highest rank. Let one
single quotation be evidence of his penetration and his
fairness:

> Le catholicisme, non en ce qui lui reste de chrétien,
> mais en ce qu'il a de spécifiquement catholique, est
> l'Eglise du *sens commun*. On croit généralement le con-
> traire, et c'est le protestantisme qui a l'air de triompher
> par le sens commun; mais il *n'en a que l'air*, car ses bases
> sont beaucoup plus idéales. Il s'est placé volontairement
> dans la position périlleuse et sublime ou de périr, s'il ne
> veut pas remonter, comme protestantisme, au delà du sens
> commun, ou de jeter ses ancres au delà du voile mysté-
> rieux (et mystique) s'il ne veut pas disparaître.

19

J. S. Phillimore's *Some Remarks on Translation and Translators*

It is a thousand times pity that so vivid and provocative a paper as that of Professor Phillimore on "Translation and Translators" should be condemned to the comparative obscurity of the transactions of the English Association. It may be that the Association is, in fact, a realm where a great light is shed, and every inhabitant mind is stimulated by the repercussions of so lively a debate. But I have had a small experience of the Association in session, and I have my doubts. A little while ago I heard Mr. John Drinkwater lecture at the headquarters of the confraternity upon "Modern Poetry and the English Tradition," or some such subject. The lecture was received, as far as I could judge, with rapt attention; but at no point was the discreet undercurrent of applause more explosive than at a properly superior comparison of the activities of certain ultra-modern experimenters in poetry to the Bolsheviks. I could swear that Mr. Drinkwater deliberately baited his hook. I could not have mistaken the significance of his suave and confident pause when he set the word "anarchy" rolling round the amphitheatre, and, I confess, I conceived a certain admiration of his platform skill. Mr. Drinkwater evidently knew his audience. Indeed, there were other reasons for supposing that. I cannot imagine that he would have dared to face any but a familiar audience with an oration so jejune as

Some Remarks on Translation and Translators. By J. S. Phillimore. English Association Pamphlet No. 42. (*Athenaeum,* 2 May 1919.)

that with which he charmed the souls of the members of the Association at Gower Street. And the visible impatience with which they received the remarks of a gentleman who, instead of moving the usual perfunctory and insincere vote of thanks, sought to confront Mr. Drinkwater with a real critical problem, showed that Mr. Drinkwater's estimate of his audience was near enough to the mark.

Therefore I have some warrant for holding that Professor Phillimore's essay, being a pamphlet of the English Association, is condemned to a comparative obscurity, from which I desire, in some measure, to emancipate it. It will, in most of its parts, well support an intenser light. Its author has a mind and a judgment of his own, and, even though this welcome idiosyncrasy leads him to one monstrous enormity, it remains as gratifying as it is unfamiliar in a gentleman of his academic standing. And even his enormity serves to point a moral which I was already determined to emphasize. "When you read someone who writes good modern English, do you not say," asks Professor Phillimore, " 'This is the kind of man who ought to translate Plato' "?

> But, alas, one has to admit some impediment every time. Matthew Arnold was a prig; Shaw and Wells are buffoons, and know no Greek; Pater knew too much Greek, and perhaps wrote English too much like a foreign language. The requirements have never yet been found co-existing. Mr. Compton Mackenzie is my present favourite for the appointment.

The first social revolutionaries in English history advanced to the assault of institutions with an insidious rhyme:

> If Adam delved and Eve span,
> Who was then the gentleman?

If Arnold is a prig and Wells a buffoon, who is the gentleman of our modern letters? Certainly there is a sense in which the writer of one of the few really comic novels since the "Pickwick Papers" ("The History of

Mr. Polly") is, by the very fact, a buffoon. And there have not been many professors worthy to unloose the shoes of buffoons like these. Anyhow, the club in which Mr. Wells and Mr. Shaw can be spoken of as buffoons with impunity must be very select indeed—so select that we can imagine only one modern with the right of entry, and he is Mr. Hardy. But one thing is quite certain. If there is, as there may be, a kingdom of quiet reverie where the mind, consorting with the great dead, strips the moderns of all their ephemeral notorieties and assays the naked residue; where the sentence is given that Mr. Wells and Mr. Shaw have not enough reverence for the things that *must* be revered—in that kingdom of ultimate honesties the name of Mr. Compton Mackenzie has never been heard. Before one can enter there, he and all his works are shuffled off with the red-brick suburbia where his soul has never ceased to take delight.

But why is it that one who writes an exact and nervous, if undisciplined, prose, who has the courage to exercise an honest and individual, if unsteady, judgment among the ancient and modern idols, should so jeopardize the sympathy which we who seek to reinstate criticism were prepared to grant him? What evil genius jerked at his elbow? Or is all the keen edge of his aperçus only a delusion of our minds? The most eager apologist cannot conceal the monstrous concatenation of Plato and the author of "Sylvia and Michael." Like any crime, it will out, and we have not dared to pass over it in silence. We have no theory to explain away the aberration, though we have a desire to be informed of the attendant circumstances. What modern authors since Mr. Wells and Mr. Shaw has Professor Phillimore read? Has he read even Mr. Mackenzie in the original? Or is he content to read the newspaper criticisms? We are loth to believe this of him, but if it is true we should like to know what newspapers he reads. For if he reads the same newspapers as we do, he must have given up the practice a year ago. Otherwise, he would be aware that a greater than Mr. Mackenzie has arisen, one still more adequate to give us an English "Philebus"—in the person of Mr. Hugh Walpole.

And yet, and yet (as Mr. W. B. Yeats has lately sung), there is, undeniably, a great deal of excellent sense elsewhere in Professor Phillimore's paper. He will, for instance, have nothing to do with the neo-barbarism "Foreword"; he stoutly (and most truly) maintains that:

> In Latin prose it is simply true to say that St. Jerome and St. Augustine could drive their ship under all the sail that ever Cicero carried. To call them a decadence is a foolish prejudice only possible to those who never read them. The inspiration is new, but no new expressive power is needed. They inherited that. Expressiveness in prose was maintained for nearly five centuries by the Latins: from Cicero to Augustine is a table-land on the high level.

Or he is admirably suggestive, as when, in insisting on the importance of the translator "estimating the pitch" of the author he translates—would that a diabolical little Beerbohm picture of Mr. Mackenzie estimating the pitch of the "Republic" did not interpose between our eye and the paper!—he asserts that an understanding of Servius's remark on the fourth Aeneid (*"poene comicus est stilus"*) is a touchstone for the translator of Virgil. Or he is simple and wise:

> Those are the happiest ages when a man writes the language of his time, having no necessity or temptation to do otherwise. Under these conditions even second-rate talent has a career open to attain distinguished success. For frugality is so much a note of true classicism—and these conditions are those of classicism—that not merely the individual, but also the community economises. Its inheritance is improved. For the great men's use of language leaves it more efficacious for smaller men coming after them to employ well; whereas your Dervish Contortionists, the Strong men or Supermen of literature—I will instance Carlyle—leave a track of destruction behind them. Our language is an instrument which their wilful-

ness has abused and left less fit for the next workman. Everyone will write better for taking a course of Swift, Hazlitt, or Newman, or other writers of "central" prose; but a course of Carlyle will merely betray itself in certain nervous tricks of outlandish grimaces.

Professor Phillimore's arguments are—as he freely acknowledges—not very tightly buttoned. His essay is rather notes for a book than an essay. But the final sentence of this quotation brings us back to one of his main theses, that translation is the chief exercise by which a language is brought to increasing flexibility and expressiveness. It is an interesting thesis, persuasive *a priori*, and in some cases (for example, the French) demonstrably true in fact. But will it hold of English itself? At the first glance it does. The splendours of rhythm and resonance, the subtleties of emotional significance of the "Areopagitica" are largely due, not indeed to the exercise of actual translation, but to one analogous to it. Yet is Milton's in any sense "central" prose? On the other hand, Dryden's prose is "central" beyond a doubt, and Dryden gave us the most adequate translation of Virgil we possess. But Bunyan's prose stands still nearer the node and true centre of the English prose tradition, and he had no truck with the classics. He forged his own instrument out of the common speech, elucidated native rhythms and gave a compactness to its texture that not even Dryden could achieve. And Defoe? And Swift himself? Were they indebted to translators?

Let Professor Phillimore argue his own case for England. It is worth argument and debate, and on the whole, current criticism has much to gain if the resolute custodians of the old descend to parley with the guardians of the new. He may find that what he is after and what we desire are nearly the same. We were convinced it was so until we alighted upon that unhappy dictum concerning Plato and another. Perhaps the unfamiliar riot of what has happily been called our Great Exhibition confused him on his previous descent. He went into a side-show and saw a live lion. We, *habitués,* could have told him that it was only stuffed; we could have told him how it was stuffed and with what. But if he would make the next journey with us we could show him a few real things, and we would listen to his opinion of them with interest.

III Mystics

20

H. P. Blavatsky's *Isis Unveiled*

In 1889 Madame Blavatsky, while publicly correcting a mistake in *Isis Unveiled* over which an exaggerated fuss had been made, concluded her correction with the words: "The work was written in exceptional circumstances, and no doubt more than one great error may be discovered in *Isis Unveiled*." Her candour was admirable; in face of it, for a modern reader of her work to insist on dubious points of detail would be worse than ungracious. There was in Madame Blavatsky herself a largeness of nature, and in her work a comprehensiveness which forestalls by anticipation all trivial and pedantic criticism. It is but simple justice to recognise that the composition of *Isis Unveiled* was an astonishing achievement.

It was written in a bare two years, in the midst of engrossing activities. As a mere piece of composition, the writing of these two large volumes now made accessible in one was a formidable task. As a comprehensive collection of material of every kind and quality, the work was prodigious. And when we consider that the audience to which it was immediately addressed consisted almost exclusively of spiritists, whom we know to be rather more impervious than mechanical materialists to spirit-

Isis Unveiled: A Master-Key to the Mysteries of Ancient and Modern Science and Theology. Centenary Anniversary Edition. Two volumes bound in one. The Theosophy Co., Los Angeles, California. (*Aryan Path*, January 1932.)

ual truth, and that Madame Blavatsky was addressing them in a language not her own, we must allow that the circumstances in which the work was written were something more than "exceptional." They might fairly be called unique.

From my own quite personal point of view, there are two main elements in *Isis Unveiled*, of which one, I must frankly confess, makes no appeal to me whatever. These two elements are, first, the insistence, with a wealth of supporting evidence, on the essential truth and fundamental identity of all high religions; and, second, the endeavour to convince the public of the reality of occult powers. For some reason or other, I have never been able to take even a faint interest in occultism. I have never been sufficiently interested even to be sceptical of the astonishing phenomena said to be produced by Eastern "adepts"; to me these belong to the same order as the miracles of the New Testament. Whether or not they really occur is indifferent to me, because they seem to me irrelevant to that spirituality which I hold to be of supreme worth. Occult phenomena—of which I have absolutely no experience—would never be to me the evidence of spirituality. In this matter, the truth, as I understand it, was spoken for all time by St. Paul.

> And though I have prophecy, and know all the mysteries and all the gnosis, and though I have all the faith so as to be able to remove mountains, but have not love, I am nothing.

St. Paul, of course, definitely believed in the reality of occult powers, and probably set great store by their possession; but they seemed to him of no account beside the spiritual rebirth which, in his language, was described as "being possessed by Christ"—not by the individual and historical person, but the eternal spirit which was manifest in him.

Madame Blavatsky's real attitude in this matter in *Isis Unveiled* I find hard to grasp. Towards the end of the second volume (p. 634) she writes:

By those who have followed us thus far, it will naturally be asked, to what practical issue this book tends; much has been said about magic and its potentiality, much of the immense antiquity of its practice. Do we wish to affirm that the occult sciences ought to be studied and practised throughout the world? Would we replace modern spiritualism with the ancient magic? Neither; the substitution could not be made, nor the study universally prosecuted, without incurring the risk of enormous public dangers . . .

We would have neither scientists, theologians, nor spiritualists turn practical magicians, but all to realize that there was true science, profound religion, and genuine phenomena before this modern era. We would that all who have a voice in the education of the masses should first know and then *teach* that the safest guides to human happiness and enlightenment are those writings which have descended to us from the remotest antiquity; and that nobler spiritual aspirations and a higher average morality prevail in the countries where the people take their precepts as the rule of their lives. We would have all to realize that magical, *i.e.*, spiritual powers exist in every man, and those few to practise them who feel called to teach, and are ready to pay the price of discipline and self-conquest which their development exacts.

Here, I must confess myself completely non-plussed by this simple equating of the magical and the spiritual. Whether or not spiritual powers are ever connected with magical powers (of which, unfortunately, I know nothing), I am convinced that there is no *necessary* connexion between them.

This may be simple ignorance on my part; but it is indurated and apparently unchangeable. Therefore it is not in the insistence upon and the evidence for the reality of magical powers that I find the main importance of *Isis Unveiled*. Madame Blavatsky herself came to lay less stress upon them; and she wrote, in *Five Messages*, that "the ethics of Theosophy are more important than any divulgement of psychic laws and facts." Her great achievement, in my opinion, was the simultaneous onslaught which she made on the deadly enemies of true spirituality. On the one side she conducted a vigorous and victorious criticism of scientific materialism. At the time she wrote materialism was rampant. To the ordinary educated Western man there appeared, in the 1870's, to be but two alternatives: conventional religious orthodoxy, and mechanical materialism. Madame Blavatsky smote both the one and the other. As against the merely biological evolutionists, she insisted on the simple fact that the Life outside ourselves which Science examines is but the corpse of Life. The only place where Life can be immediately and truly known is in the soul of man. As against the religious sectarians, she pointed triumphantly to the universally valid spiritual knowledge enshrined from times immemorial in the sacred wisdom of India.

To this twofold effect roughly corresponds her division of her work into two volumes: the first, Science; the second, Theology. As against the narrowness of so-called Science, she maintains, in accordance with the highest philosophical tradition of East and West, that the most important of the sciences is the science of the human soul; and that this science is not, as crude scepticism would assert, unattainable. On the contrary it really exists, and has existed for ages; it has always been the substance of lofty religions, and that substance has always been identical with itself. What has varied is the mode of statement, the necessary imperfection that attaches to the utterance of the unutterable. This imperfection changes from being external and accidental, and becomes inward and essential, so soon as any particular statement of the universal and eternal truth claims for itself exclusive validity. On p. 639 of *Isis Unveiled* (Vol. II) she writes:

> Our examination of the multitudinous religious faiths that mankind, early and late, have professed, most assuredly indicates that they have all been derived from one primitive source. It would seem as if they were all but different modes of expressing the yearning of the impris-

oned human soul for intercourse with supernal spheres. As
the white ray of light is decomposed by the prism into the
various colors of the solar spectrum, so the beam of divine
Truth, in passing through the *three-sided* prism of man's
nature, has been broken up into vari-colored fragments
called RELIGIONS. And as the rays of the spectrum, by
imperceptible shadings, merge into each other, so the
great theologies that have appeared at different degrees of
divergence from the original source, have been connected
by minor schisms, schools, and off-shoots from the one
side or the other. Combined, their aggregate represents
one eternal Truth; separate, they are but shades of human
error and the signs of imperfection.

That is Madame Blavatsky at her best. The truth she
utters is vital, and the expression is admirable, even in
detail. One observes the particular emphasis on the
three-fold nature of man. This conception—which is, I
think, fundamental to high religion—is expounded in
two remarkable chapters on Christianity in Vol. II (pp.
123–209). (It should be said, in passing, that Madame
Blavatsky's discernment of the part played by Gnosti-
cism in the early Christian Church, and her rehabilita-
tion of Marcion against traditional denigration have
been since amply confirmed by unbiassed scholarship.)
She insists on the indubitable fact that Jesus never
claimed for himself a position of privilege with regard to
God. He was indeed and claimed to be "the son of
God," never "the only son of God." To represent him as
making this claim is to make nonsense of his teaching, of
which the all-important article was that men should
learn how to become "sons of God." When, therefore,
he became, for the author of the Fourth Gospel, "the
only begotten son of God," the historical Jesus had been
lost in the eternal Christ: "begotten of his Father, *before
all worlds*." There is truth in both conceptions. It is thus
expressed by Madame Blavatsky:

"God's son" is the immortal spirit assigned to every
human being. It is this divine entity which is the "*only
man*," for the casket which contains our soul, and the soul

itself, are but half entities, and without its overshadowing both body and astral soul, the two are but an animal duad. It requires a trinity to form the complete "man." (II. 195.)

This is the true significance of the Christian mystery of "the undwelling Christ." By following the true teaching of Jesus—utterly distinct from the compromises and distortions of church Christianity—at all times men have attained what Jesus told them they would attain: the sense of being "sons of God." Thereby, they have attained veritable communion with the Jesus who showed them the path; but not with the personal Jesus, rather with the impersonal and omnipresent spiritual reality to which he attained, and in which he eternally lives. To this realm of reality belong by an equal title all the great masters of religion.

This is the veritable world of spirit. It is, and must be, impersonal. As a brilliant writer in the September number of THE ARYAN PATH (p. 653) puts it:

> SELF is not personal; Law is not personal; action is not personal; nature is not personal; only *human* nature is personal. This is so because only in mankind is the threefold evolution, Spiritual, Intellectual, Physical, conjoined, albeit not yet *identified* as one and the same SELF in all. SELF is *impersonal* in every man, as in all Nature.

Self, in this supreme sense, is the final discovery of Spirit. True Self and true Spirit are given together. In the world of Spirit alone does universal brotherhood become reality, although this "becoming" is but an effect of perspective due to our own immersion in the sensual flux. The process of "becoming" is the process of the liberation of our impersonal self from the flux. The impersonal self is eternal; and it knows, simply and immediately, that universal brotherhood is not an ideal, but a fact. Our struggle to attain to knowledge of this fact may be arduous; but the fact is lucid and unchanging. Our personal reality, if we will but inquire diligently into the nature and submit ourselves humbly to *all* experience that comes to us, leads us directly to a reality which is impersonal, yet most truly ours. This is our veritable essence; and this essence, once known, is known to be of one spiritual substance with the essences of all men and all things, past, present and to come.

This doctrine, which I believe to be true, was presented by Madame Blavatsky more fully in *The Secret Doctrine*. In *Isis Unveiled*, she was content with a more cursory statement. But the second and third articles of her "fundamental propositions" in Chapter XII, Vol. II (p. 587) are perfectly definite:

> 2d. Nature is triune: there is a visible, objective nature; an invisible, indwelling, energizing nature, the exact model of the other, and its vital principle; and, above these two, *spirit*, source of all forces, alone eternal, and indestructible. The lower two constantly change; the higher third does not.
>
> 3d. Man is also triune: he has his objective, physical body; his vitalizing astral body (or soul), the real man; and these two are brooded over and illuminated by the third—the sovereign, the immortal spirit. When the real man succeeds in merging himself with the latter, he becomes an immortal entity.

There is to me in this nothing occult, nothing magical. It is simply spiritual truth. I might express it somewhat differently; but it is in the nature of things spiritual that the same eternal truth should be capable of being expressed differently in terms of different individual experience. If it is occult and magical, then I must be something of an occultist and a magician without knowing it. Occult, in the sense of being concealed for many, of course it is. Wisdom is not to be had for nothing.

> What is the price of Experience? Do men
>   buy it for a song,
> Or wisdom for a dance in the street? No, it
>   is bought with the price
> Of all that a man hath—his house, his wife,
>   his children.

> Wisdom is sold in the desolate market where
>   none come to buy,
> And in the wither'd field where the farmer
>   plows for bread in vain.

William Blake's moving and beautiful words find their response in every man who has learned a little by suffering. Wisdom is always incomprehensible to those who lack the experience which precedes it.

But this incomprehensible quality of wisdom is not what is ordinarily understood by "occult." And here is my chief grievance against *Isis Unveiled*. As it would be ungracious to insist on dubious details, so it would be dishonest in me to conceal a more essential dissatisfaction. I regret that Madame Blavatsky allowed herself so frequently to be turned aside from her work of exposition of spiritual truths. That is, at best, no easy task; but it seems to me that Madame Blavatsky complicated it enormously by her addiction to mystery. Spiritual truth is mysterious; but it is also simple. The parables of Jesus, the sayings of Buddha—these are mysterious, but they are not complicated. One does not have the feeling, in their presence, that enormous labours, prodigious journeys, strange initiations, are necessary before they can be comprehended. Or take the wonderful description of Yoga from the *Bhagavad-Gita*, lately quoted in these pages by Professor Sarma:

> That in which the mind is at rest restrained by the practice of concentration, that in which he beholds the spirit through the mind and rejoices in the spirit;
> That in which he knows the boundless joy beyond the reach of the senses and grasped only by the understanding, and that in which when he is established, he never departs from Truth;
> That on gaining which he feels there is no greater gain, and that in which he abides and is not moved even by the heaviest of afflictions—
> Let that be known as Yoga.

To such spiritual purity we respond immediately, or not at all. If we respond, we *know* that this blessed condition is within our reach. We have but to look steadily within ourselves, mortifying and rejecting from our essence all that is the false, material self. We do not need to compass earth and sea; we do not need vast knowledge, or strange encounters, only the unshakeable determination to reach the truth of our own inward being. That is hard; but it is not hard in the way Madame Blavatsky too often makes the quest for truth appear in *Isis Unveiled*.

I do not mean that a man can travel the path altogether alone. That would be quite false to my own small experience. I owe the great masters an infinite debt. When I groped after the meaning of my own experience, I found it uttered by them. The masters of East and West have equally been my guides. But they have been masters open to all: books you can buy for half-a-crown. I have never felt the need of any more secret doctrine; nor do I really believe that, if there is a more secret doctrine, it is a whit more truly spiritual than the doctrine open to all.

Therefore, I am out of sympathy with Madame Blavatsky's tendency to make a mundane mystery of things that are mysterious only because they are spiritual. It seems to me that this tendency disfigures *Isis Unveiled*, and to it I attribute another great defect: that it is a baffling and disordered book. There is no steady progress to a conclusion, no gradual gathering of the manifold into simplicity, no final illumination. Everywhere there are flashes of true insight, passages of wisdom; but they disappear. To me, speaking as an unbiassed critic, it is as though *Isis Unveiled* were the work of one who had not yet truly made up her mind. That is not astonishing, considering the immense mass of material she handled and the short time she had to deal with it. But it prevents me from regarding the book with the same unqualified admiration as others to whom the works of Madame Blavatsky are as scriptures.

21

Jesus and the Essenes

The substance of Mr. George Moore's novel, *The Brook Kerith*, is not entirely new. One hundred and fifty years ago Karl Friedrich Bahrdt had imagined that Jesus of Nazareth had emerged from the order of the Essenes to fulfil his mission and returned to it after a seeming death; he was followed by Venturini, whose *Natural History of the Great Prophet of Nazareth* (1800) —a remarkable book—is based on the same supposition. After these came Salvator and Gfrörer, Nahor and Bosc. There is, in fact, a whole sequence of imaginative lives of Jesus based upon the hypothesis in which, to many readers, lay the originality of Mr. George Moore's novel.

Modern critical scholarship, as usual, frowns on the notion. We may take as characteristic the remark of Professor James Moffatt: "At one time ingenious attempts were made to trace the affinities of the Essenes with the early Christians. . . . It is no longer necessary to prove that Jesus was not an Essene, and that early Christianity was not Essenic." One wonders how that negative proposition could be *proved*. But this peremptory assurance comes easy to some Biblical scholars, who would be pained and shocked if an equal rigour of negative scepticism were applied to their own religious assumptions. All that scholarship is entitled to affirm is that there is no definite evidence that Jesus was an Essene.

Aryan Path, May 1931.

We may say, if we like, that the authors of the "ficti-tious" lives of Jesus, from Bahrdt to Moore, have been the victims of a wild imagination; but in matters of religion a wild imagination is better than no imagination at all. Imagination is always necessary if fact is to be transmuted into truth. Imagination may degenerate into mere fantasy; on the other hand, a certain measure of fantasy is necessary to the expression of imaginative truth. And it seems to me that the soberest mind, reflect-ing on the actual facts, must be prepared to entertain the possibility, or even the probability, of a connection of some kind between Jesus and the Essenes.

The facts are these. First, that Jesus of Nazareth was one of the world's greatest religious and ethical teachers. If the word "spiritual master" means anything, he was one. Moreover, he was essentially a mystic, a teacher of the necessity of a mystical, or spiritual "rebirth." In spiritual insight, in the perfection of his tolerance, he towered above the ordinary religious Jews of his time. Second, it so happened that at this particular moment in the world's history there was, in Palestine, a very aston-ishing order of religious Jews called the Essenes; there was also in Egypt, living among the low hills to the south of Lake Mareotis, an equally astonishing order of religious Jews called the Therapeutae. The evidence for the existence of these orders is incontrovertible; they are, in actual fact, better attested than the early Christians themselves. If we knew as much about the primitive Church as we do about the Essenes and the Therapeu-tae, half at least of the historical problems of Christian-ity would be solved out of hand. We insist again that it is at the precise moment of history when Jesus appeared that these two orders also appear.

It is to Philo, who was after Jesus, and perhaps a little, but very little, after Paul, the most remarkable Jew of his time, that we owe our main knowledge of these two orders. Philo commemorated them, because he so im-mensely admired and venerated them. Moreover, they justified his passionate belief in the possibility of Juda-ism rising to the level of a universal religion. He compares the Essenes to the Persian magi or the Indian gymnosophists; of the Therapeutae he says that "they are part of a movement which is known outside Egypt." To the Essenes, moreover, we have the testimony of the awe-struck Pliny: "Strange to say, the race has lasted for untold ages (*per milia saeculorum*) though no one is born within it." It is "a race more remarkable than any other in the wide world." Josephus, whose detailed account of the Essenes is very impressive, lived in their neighbourhood for three years as the *chela* of Banus the anchorite, who appears to have been at one time an Essene himself.

There is more than one distinction to be made between the Essenes and the Therapeutae; but it seems extravagant to deny that there must have been some close connection between them. The connection is probable on general grounds, seeing that both the orders were Jewish, and that the connection between Egypt and Palestine was intimate; the probability is heightened immeasurably when we consider that their doctrines were alike esoteric, and that both interpreted their sacred books—which certainly included more than the canonical scriptures—by allegory and symbolism; and it becomes a practical certainty when we find that Philo, to whom we owe our only account of the Therapeutae, describes the Essenes as the "therapeutae" of God. The associations of the particular word were well-known to him.

If we regard, as we must, Jesus of Nazareth as the great religious seeker of his nation and his time, it is very difficult to believe that he was not merely conscious, but acutely aware, of the existence of these orders. Their observances and doctrines were far nearer to his own teaching than were those of the early Christian Church. The Essenes and the Therapeutae alike were far beyond the point at which an unseemly wrangle over the necessity of circumcision could convulse them. The Essenes repudiated sacrifice and the doctrine of sacrifice. (The doctrine of the sacrifice of Jesus himself as a propitiation

for men's sins, one need not insist, is a crude posthumous invention that is utterly alien to the teaching of
Jesus himself.) The Essenes practised the love that
Jesus taught; their life, says Philo, "gives proofs of an
indescribable bond of fellowship." They held that the
master-slave relation was a violation of the order of Nature; they lived on terms of perfect amity and equality
with one another, practising peaceful arts, and giving
their earnings to a common store. There was, however, a
hierarchy of rank among them, according to the length
of years they had served in the order. They were an
ascetic order; though Josephus tells us that there was a
branch of them which did not eschew marriage: and we
gather from Philo that for an Essene to have children
was not exceptional. But on his entry into the strict
order he said farewell to marriage. The order consisted in
the main of mature men, though it was partly recruited
by the adoption of chosen youths.

"It is no longer necessary to prove that Jesus was not
an Essene." After the recital of these uncontroverted
facts, Dr. Moffatt's words begin to bear a sense opposite
to that which he intended. It is surely mere prejudice
which would deny the high probability that Jesus was at
least deeply influenced by this remarkable order. In this
matter, at least, Madame Blavatsky's contentions in *Isis
Unveiled* are far more reasonable than the unimaginative negations of dry as dust scholars who can never
persuade themselves that Jesus was a human being at all.
The truth is that he *could not* have been ignorant of the
Essenes; and if there is such a thing as psychological
probability, he must have been curious and eager about
them, and he must have sought contact with them. They
were, like himself, heretics among the Jews, and it is
highly probable that their disappearance from the pages
of history is due to an outburst of that frenzied Jewish
fanaticism which was so grimly punished by Titus.

Nor would it have been difficult for Jesus to make
contact with them. Relatively, the Essenes were numerous. They numbered 4000, while of the Pharisees them-

selves there were only 6000. There were two Essenes to every three Pharisees in Judaea. And though it is probable that the majority of the Essenes lived in desert communities, the testimony of Josephus is quite definite that "large numbers of them inhabit every city." These city communities were well organised; each had "a special relieving-officer for strangers," whose business it was to provide the wanderer with food and shelter. Again, the reasonable supposition is that it would have been impossible for Jesus to avoid coming into contact with them.

To leave aside for the moment the question of their actual doctrines, the reader of the accounts in Philo and Josephus is impressed by two distinct characteristics in their practices. On the one hand the emphasis of their daily ritual was upon purification. Thus the novice, on entering the order, was given "a sort of spade." No doubt this tool served many purposes, and was in some sort a symbol of their social activity, but the purpose on which Josephus insists was that the Essene used it for digging a hole into which he eased himself; afterwards he performed a ritual ablution. The Essenes partook of a ceremonial midday meal and supper together, for which they clad themselves in white linen robes. Every day they bathed themselves in water, and the crucial stages in the progress of the novice, (who had to serve one year's probation, then a further period of two years, before he became a full member of the order) were marked by a ritual bathing. On the other hand, though the emphasis on purification was so great, the Essenes did not withdraw from society. They worked at their various crafts among ordinary men, and received their wages which they paid into the common store. They were not contemplative anchorites, but practical mystics who acknowledged their social obligations. Hence it is not surprising, as Josephus says, that they did not "repudiate marriage with its function of carrying on the race," or that there was a branch of the order which was composed of men still living with their wives. The majority of the Essenes appear to have been men who had got "beyond marriage," rather than men in principle opposed to it.

For their actual doctrine, which was obviously esoteric, we have to rely on a few words of Josephus, and certain unavoidable implications. Josephus says that they believed in the eternality of the human soul, which they regarded as being in bondage to the flesh. He also says that the novice, on being finally received into the order, "swears to communicate their principles precisely as he himself received them . . . and to preserve with like care the sacred books of the society and the names of the angels." The "names of the angels" powerfully suggests the Gnostic belief in the successive emanation from the eternal and uncreated Godhead, of *Nous*, of the *Logos*, of the divine Intelligences (or Angels), and of the Sophia (or Wisdom of God). That their doctrines were Gnostic is borne out by Philo's admiration of the Essenes, and by the evidence that the greater part of their lore was symbolic. Probably, like the Therapeutae, they used the Jewish scriptures simply as matter for allegorical interpretation. Again the total repudiation of sacrifice, by which they separated themselves as absolutely from contemporary Judaism as a modern Catholic would separate himself from his Church by repudiating the Mass, suggests forcibly that their doctrines were truly spiritual. Their ceremonial, in turn, suggests that they had a profound belief in the doctrine of "the eternal rebirth of the soul" which, in one form or another, has always been central to mysticism. That their "newness of life" was real and striking is beyond all doubt.

Did such an order spring up spontaneously in the heart of Judaism? It is possible. Ultimately the doctrines of all truly spiritual religions are the same, and the spontaneous generation of a universal spiritual wisdom would only be another witness to the fundamental identity of the human soul. At the same time, although it is possible that the Essenes represented a completely independent movement, it is not probable. The Roman province of Syria, of which Judaea was a part, was the des-

tined place of meeting between the religious ideas of the
East and West. It seems to me highly probable that the
Essenes owed their very distinctive character to the influence of Buddhism; and further that Madame Blavatsky
was well within the bounds of historical probability
when she maintained that, through the Essenes, Jesus
himself was deeply influenced in his ethical and spiritual
teaching by some of the purest spiritual doctrine of the
East.

As a matter of "scientific" history—if true history can
ever be really "scientific"—the supposition is not necessary. But the sheer historical probability of the influence
is great, greater far than the ordinary Biblical scholar will
admit. Whether we shall turn a high probability into a
certainty depends, not on the facts themselves which are
so few that they offer no resistance to an imaginative
interpretation, but rather on our temper and purposes.
Madame Blavatsky's temper and purposes were such that
in this matter she was a better historian than the academic sceptics. She had deep religious experience, and a
great power of imaginative sympathy; and she knew for a
fact that all high religions are in essence identical. *And
that is a fact.* She also knew that the human soul, in its
own religious progress, eagerly seeks out sustenance for
itself and corroboration of its own experience wherever it
can find it; and naturally she could not believe that Jesus
of Nazareth was any exception to the rule. Whether he
was actually taught as a boy by the Essenes, as Mr.
George Moore, following Venturini, imagines, or
whether when his own religious experience became more
definite he sought for confirmation of it among them—
such a question is of course beyond our decision. But
that the influence of the purest religion of the East was
there among the Essenes, that Jesus would naturally
have sought to avail himself of it, and that he did avail
himself of it—these are probabilities with a better title to
be called certainties than a good many articles of the
Christian faith.

22

Philo and the Therapeutae

The historical origins of the Christian Church are lost in obscurity. There seems never to have been a time when they were not hidden. The first authentic Christian document we possess—Paul's Epistle to the Thessalonians—reveals to us a Church already in being, but one established by a man who had not known Jesus of Nazareth after the flesh, and believing in doctrines different from those taught by Jesus himself. In twenty or thirty years a discredited and crucified prophet had become a deity; and of the process of that mighty transmutation we know almost nothing. The Fathers of the Church knew no more than we.

Accordingly, when in the third century Eusebius of Caesarea, the first and greatest historian of the Christian Church, came across the treatise of Philo Judaeus on *The Contemplative Life* which gave an obviously trustworthy account of a remarkable order of Greek-speaking Jews who early in the first century had separated themselves from the great world of Alexandria, divested themselves of their possessions, and lived a life of austerity and contemplation, he promptly and very naturally decided that he had discovered some early Christians. And so for many centuries, indeed almost to within modern times, the Therapeutae of Lake Mareotis in Egypt were adopted into the Christian tradition.

Aryan Path, September 1931.

They did not belong to it, any more than the Essenes belonged to it. Both were independent communities which were in existence before Jesus of Nazareth was born. What resemblances they had to the early Christians derived from the fact that their beliefs, like those of Jesus himself, were genuinely spiritual, and from the fact that the ostensible parent of the Therapeutae, the Essenes and the Christians alike was Judaism. But the Judaism from which the Therapeutae and the Essenes also were descended was a Judaism that had undergone contact not merely with Greek thought, but probably also with the wisdom of the East. It was specifically the Judaism of Alexandria, at once the great centre of Hellenistic civilisation and the chief gateway between the West and East. Of this symbolic Judaism Philo was, if not the master, the great apostle; and Philo profoundly admired the Therapeutae, who were if anything a little nearer and dearer to him even than the Essenes, because they were a living example of the religion which he devotedly professed.

Essentially, this religion was a mystical Judaism liberated from literalness and local accident. It was, by intention and in fact (for there were moments when it seemed likely to become the creed of the élite of the Roman world) a universal religion. Philo, and the Alexandrian Jews of his persuasion, liberated themselves from the shackles of a literal interpretation of the Hebrew Scriptures in precisely the same way as some of the greatest of Christian mystics were to liberate themselves in subsequent centuries, namely by the method of allegorical interpretation. This was the method of Paracelsus and Böhme and William Blake; and the tradition was maintained throughout the Middle Ages in Europe by the Kabbalists. And, provided that the method is never suffered to degenerate into a new formalism—a danger that can only be warded off by the reality of personal spiritual experience to vivify the symbols—it is a precious means to deeper understanding. Again, the Jews of Philo's persuasion liberated themselves by having received deep into their minds the fundamental mystical idea that all religions are one. This seemed to them to be corroborated even in detail by the correspondence between the Old Testament, allegorically interpreted, and the doctrines of Pythagoras and Plato. They had no doubt—and the most enlightened modern scholarship equally has no doubt—that the central doctrines of Platonism were derived from Pythagoras. The belief in a divine harmony of the universe, with which it was the duty of the individual man to become attuned by achieving a like harmony in himself, was confirmed for Pythagoras by his discovery of the relations between the sides of the perfect right-angled triangle. This "divine" correspondence, which is fundamental to the thought of Plato's *Timaeus*, was equally significant to the Therapeutae. Says Philo:

> They gather together every seven weeks, for they revere not only the simple week of seven days, but its power (*i.e.* its numerical square) as well. For they know it is holy and ever virgin. This is a preliminary to the greatest festival which falls to the fiftieth day, because fifty is the holiest and most natural of numbers, being composed of the power of the right-angled triangle, which is the source of the birth of all things.

It is clear to me that Philo is not here giving his own symbolic interpretation of the chosen festival of the Therapeutae, but expounding their own teaching of its significance. It is a simple and striking example of the synthesis between Greek and Hebrew mystical symbolism which the Therapeutae had achieved. And indeed in the minds of those who attached importance to such things, such a synthesis imposed itself. The relation between the sacred Hebrew number seven and the Pythagorean three and four was manifest. 50 was the sum of the squares of the sides of the Pythagorean triangle. Seven times seven is forty-nine. These correspondences may seem trivial to a modern mind. We need a certain power of imagination to transport ourselves to the time when the Pythagorean proposition, and the harmonies connected with it, seemed to afford a direct glimpse into the structure of the universe, and to be palpable evidence of a fundamental harmony in all things to which mortal men could penetrate in so far as they achieved a kindred harmony in themselves. To this noble and profound philosophy the Therapeutae, like the Pythagoreans, adhered.

They are rightly called Therapeutae, says Philo. The word in Greek has a twofold meaning. It means both "healer" and "god-worshipper." They are called by this name, says Philo, "either because they profess an art of medicine of a nobler kind than that now in vogue in great cities: there the doctors heal the body only, these the soul also. Or it is because they have been educated to worship Being itself, which is mightier than the Good, purer than the One, and older than the Monad." (The Monad, thus distinguished from the One, is the Platonic "idea" or "form" of unity: the "oneness" in which a multitude of single objects all participate.) In such a conception of the Godhead we have passed far away from the tribal deity of Israel. Yet wisely, like Philo himself, the Therapeutae attached great importance to their own observation of the Jewish law; it was precious to them, because they knew its inward meaning:

> The whole body of the Law appears to these men to be like a living animal, whose body is the literal commands or precepts, and the unseen meaning lying within the words is the soul. And in the thinking of this very thought the reasonable soul of man begins particularly to contemplate what belongs properly to itself, beholding as in a mirror the surpassing beauties of the ideas contained in the words.

Like the Essenes, the Therapeutae possessed a body of esoteric doctrine, particularly in regard to the arcane meaning of the Old Testament, of which the Law is a part. "They have," says Philo, "writings of men of old time, who were the founders of the brotherhood and have left behind them many memorials of the real ideas wrapped up in these allegories." It seems probable, therefore, that some portion at least of the Kabalistic wisdom derives from or through the Therapeutae.

Philo distinguishes between the Essenes and the Therapeutae in one cardinal respect: whereas the Essenes cultivated the practical life in all its aspects, the Therapeutae were completely given to the life of contemplation. And to this distinction corresponded a great difference in the recruiting of the two brotherhoods. The Essenes often adopted their novices as boys and were mainly a celibate community; the Therapeutae were composed entirely of men and women who had passed the prime of life. They did not simply abandon their property; they made it over legally to their heirs: for which Philo approves them. "They make others happy by their generous liberality and themselves by their philosophy." Evidently, we are to regard them as a body of wealthy and highly civilized Greek Jews who, in middle age, withdrew themselves from life in one of the great cities of the world; and it is fairly clear that to be received as a member of the Therapeutae was itself no mean distinction. It meant that the elected member had proved himself worthy to lead the contemplative life; no romantic youthful impulse to withdrawal would suffice to secure admission. Philo, indeed, is intensely critical of premature vocation: "to pass one's days with evil is most harmful," he says of young men, "but to pass them with the perfect good (*i.e.* in the contemplative life) most deceptively dangerous."

Fifty, says, Philo, is the age for retirement. But the life of the Therapeutae was so austere that it would have been too hard for those who were not prepared for it. To be received into the order was evidently the culmination rather than the beginning of a spiritual life. Each member lived in a little hut, divided into two rooms, in one of which he lived; while the other served as a sanctuary "in which the mysteries of the holy life are performed by each in solitude." They ate neither food nor drink till sunset, when they partook of plain bread with salt or hyssop. They had no other food than this at any time. For six days they remained solitary within their houses spending the whole time between their morning and evening prayer in the practice of their philosophy, that is, in silent meditation on the hidden meaning of the Scriptures, or in the composition of "lyric songs and hymns to God." On the seventh day they met together, and listened in silence to an address from "the oldest and most experienced in their doctrines." On every forty-ninth day they met with special solemnity as a preliminary to the great festival of the 50th day. After raising their eyes and hands to heaven, they reclined in the order of their election to the brotherhood, the men on the right, the women on the left, and partook of a solemn meal of bread and water served to them by the most recent members. Afterwards they sang an antiphon and danced a choric dance, based on the song of Miriam, commemorating the deliverance of Israel from Egypt by the passing of the Red Sea. Philo tells us elsewhere that this deliverance is symbolic of the liberation of the Soul from the bondage of worldly cares.

These are most of the facts concerning the Therapeutae recorded by Philo. He asserts that they are "part of a movement that is known outside Egypt"; and, apart from the fact that his own authority is of the best, it is intrinsically probable that a movement of this kind should have been widespread. The consolidation of the Roman Empire, the complete establishment of the *pax Romana*, had made withdrawal from the shelter of great cities practically possible; while the astonishing speed with which Christianity permeated the Roman world shows that the moment was propitious for a new florescence of spiritual religion. There is a good deal of evidence to show that an enlightened Judaism had already gained many adherents in the pagan aristocracy. One must be wary of deducing too much from Philo's treatise. The connection between the Therapeutae and Pythagoreanism is evident; and possibly the Pythagorean influence is in itself enough to account for the markedly non-Jewish elements in the observances and doctrines of the Therapeutae. But Robertson-Smith, the great Biblical scholar, was convinced that there were signs of Buddhistic influence; and this is probable enough, seeing that Philo speaks elsewhere familiarly of the Indian "gymnosophoi" and gives the impression that he knew them more directly than by mere report. In any case, whether we hold the theory of direct influence or not, the resemblances between Pythagoreanism and Buddhism are striking and profound.

The significance of the Therapeutae is that, like the Essenes, they represent a singularly lofty spiritual religion, much purer and more genuinely universal than primitive Christianity. Both alike reveal a freedom from fanaticism, and above all from that utterly unspiritual pre-occupation with a future life of rewards and punishments which bulks so large in early Christianity. Madame Blavatsky was eminently justified in stressing the importance of these orders in the history of true "theosophy"; for they show how near the Western world was at the time of the birth of Jesus to a religious synthesis, and now harrowly the great opportunity was missed. Beside the Pythagorean Judaism of Philo and the Essenes and the Therapeutae, the religion of Jesus himself shines with undiminished glory; but the religion of the early Christian *Church* makes a poor showing beside it. It marked not an advance, but a spiritual retrogression. For a time, indeed, the influence of the humane tradition seems to have persisted in Alexandrian Christianity. Clement of Alexandria, who owed much to Philo, was one of the most truly spiritual of the early Fathers. But the degradation was rapid. Alexandria became the chief home of Christian fanaticism: the cock-pit where Athanasians fought with Arians and Hypatia was murdered by a pious mob.

23

Pythagoras

Towards the end of his memorable article on Pythagoras in Hastings' *Encyclopaedia of Religion and Ethics*, the late Professor Burnet made this impressive pronouncement: "It is certain that Pythagoras is entitled to be called the founder of science, and it becomes more and more clear that *all European religion and ethics, so far as they do not originate in Palestine, can also be traced back to him*." This tremendous claim for Pythagoras was made, very deliberately, by the foremost European authority on early Greek philosophy.

Of Pythagoras himself we know little; but those who have tried to gather up the slender threads which lead back to him find themselves compelled to agree with Burnet that they are approaching the presence of a very great man indeed. They have the sense of entering the field of influence of a Prometheus, of a major hero of humanity, of one of whom his followers could reasonably say what Aristotle tells us they did say: namely that there were three kinds of "rational animals": God, men, and "those like Pythagoras." And this position, midway between the divine and human, which was ascribed to Pythagoras, was, as we shall see, no mere vague extravagance of hero-worship. It corresponded definitely to the conscious effort and achievement of one of the greatest of great Europeans.

Aryan Path, November 1931.

Plato, though his work is permeated by Pythagorean influence, as Burnet has plainly proved, makes but few direct references to the Pythagoreans, and only one (in the tenth book of the *Republic*) to Pythagoras himself by name. But the reference is precious. The claims of Homer as the legendary fountain of Greek wisdom are being ruthlessly criticised by Socrates. Homer did no public good. Did he teach men privately? Did he hand on to his disciples and thence to mankind "some specific way of life as Pythagoras did, and was exceedingly loved for what he did, so that those who came after him even now call it the Pythagorean way of life, and are distinguished by it from among the rest of men?" A Way of Life—the phrase is near and dear to us to-day. It has intimate meaning for a modern seeker, as it plainly had for Plato himself. That meaning is even incorporated into the title of this magazine—the Aryan PATH.

Pythagoras gave men a Path, and was exceedingly loved for his gift to men. To the men of Greece, when Pythagoras made his discovery, it was a discovery indeed. Religion in Greece before his time, in so far as it was real, was primitive, and consisted almost solely in the performance of ritual and the observance of taboos. The Olympian deities of the northern invaders gave no scope to the religious sense at all. The scientific speculations of the early Ionians were purely materialistic and totally without bearing on the conduct of man. Pythagoras made a unity of religion and science by deepening both. The synthesis is characteristic of all that is noblest in Greek thought; to it is due the perennial power of Plato and in a less degree of Aristotle to influence the European mind. Aristotle inherited it from Plato, and Plato inherited it from Pythagoras.

What was the fundamental intuition of Pythagoras? Perhaps we can best approach it by way of his reported saying that "Life is like a great Olympic festival, to which there are three classes of visitors. Those are lowest who come to buy and sell; next above them are those who come to compete in the games; the best class however are those who come to look on." "Theōrein," the word translated "to look on," is one of the great legacies of the Greek language to European thought. "Theory" directly derives from it; but "theōria" is far more than theory: it is the contemplative understanding of detachment. To reach, by self-discipline and by study of those matters which are lifted above the flux of things, a condition of detachment and understanding and purification —this was for Pythagoras the goal towards which men should strive: by attaining it they achieved their liberation from the wheel of birth and death.

The great scientific discoveries of Pythagoras—the 47th proposition of Euclid (though probably the greater portion of the first six books of Euclid derives from him), the sphericity of the earth, and the discovery of the numerical relation of the intervals of the scale, had an immediate bearing on his religious teaching. It seemed to him evident that harmony was at the basis of reality. In the numerical relation of the intervals of the scale, by the discovery of which things apparently so different as high and low pitch were united by fixed and beautiful law, he saw a manifest solution of that conflict of opposites which so troubled early Greek speculation; and it seemed to him that this was a key to the mystery of reality. It was a kind of music, obedient to a mathematical law of harmony, divinely established. So in man himself the goal of true self-knowledge would be reached when he understood that the oppositions within himself were united by an underlying law of harmony. When this awareness was achieved he would be responsive to the harmonies of the universe. Hence came the lovely doctrine of the harmony of the spheres, or more strictly of the orbits of the planets, to which Shakespeare gave new immortality.

> Look how the floor of heaven
> Is thick inlaid with patines of bright gold:
> There's not the smallest orb which thou
>   behold'st
> But in his motion like an angel sings

Still quiring to the young-eyed cherubins;
Such harmony is in immortal souls;
But while this muddy vesture of decay
Doth grossly close it in, we cannot hear it.

That is pure Pythagoreanism; and the teaching of Pythagoras was that men must school themselves to hear the celestial and universal harmony. This is the meaning of the Pythagorean precept: "Follow God," a precept quite revolutionary in the Greece to which he spoke. By creating harmony in ourselves we become of like nature to the harmony which is divine: so, conversely, by studying the harmony which is divine we create harmony in ourselves. By this means we attain our liberation from the world of flux and conflict. Self-perfection is the true means of release. And this is manifestly concordant with the well-known reference to the esoteric doctrines of the Pythagoreans in the *Phaedo*. Socrates is surprised that Simmias and Cebes, who were exoteric disciples of Philolaus, a famous Pythagorean, have not been told the reason why it is unlawful for a man to take his own life. The esoteric doctrine is that men are in life as in a prison on parole; they must not seek to escape. Men moreover are the creatures of the Gods who are their shepherds, and they must await the signal. This may appear a simple doctrine to be called esoteric; but it has real cogency only for those who do believe that there is some underlying harmony of purpose and design in the lives of men. It is, in fact, a profound religious and ethical doctrine.

It is, at any rate in the present condition of our knowledge, impossible to distinguish clearly between the doctrines of Pythagoras himself, and those of the Pythagoreans. Nothing is more firmly established in the tradition than that Pythagoras taught a doctrine of reincarnation; but we have no means of knowing with what emphasis he taught it. Moreover, it is certain that a famous Pythagorean of the generation immediately following, Alcmæon of Croton, taught that the soul was a "harmony" of the body—a doctrine which is irreconcilable with the doctrine of reincarnation in any of its cruder forms. It seems to me that the most probable solution of the seeming discrepancy is that Pythagoras did not intend that reincarnation should be understood literally, but rather symbolically, as showing vividly the perils of remaining bound in the cycle of birth and death, and the duty laid upon men of liberating themselves from it by the effort of making themselves "like God." But this is no more than my own conjecture; and it may be that I am supersubtle in making it.*

What is reasonably certain is that within 200 years of the death of Pythagoras, his followers had become divided into two distinct branches—those who regarded him primarily as a religious leader and followed implicitly the complex "rule" of abstinences which he imparted to his disciples, and those who looked upon him chiefly as the founder of mathematical science and idealist speculation. The former, who were known as the "akousmatikoi," the followers of verbal precept, were rather despised by the latter, who were called the "mathematikoi," who appear to have resented the notion that Pythagoras was a religious teacher and to have done their best to conceal that element in his teaching. It was not easily done, for the personal prestige of Pythagoras in after years was tremendous, and immense reverence was paid to his actual words. (The "ipse dixit" is even now proverbial.) But no doubt Burnet was right in explaining the curious silence of Plato concerning Pythagoras and the Pythagoreans as due to this confusion in the ranks of his followers. "Pythagorean," at the time that Plato wrote, might mean either of two very different things: in the extreme case it might mean either a purely materialistic man of science, or a religious fanatic. And there was a still more cogent reason for Plato's reticence. It was that he himself was, in essentials, the most authentic Pythagorean of them all. The core of his own doctrine was derived from Pythagoras. And it is largely because Burnet appreciated this derivation of Plato from Pythag-

* Since this was written, I find that I was anticipated in this conjecture by Madame Blavatsky (*Isis Unveiled*, I, 291).

oras that he was moved to make the tremendous claim for Pythagoras which was quoted at the beginning of this essay. The great saying of the Platonic Socrates, that "philosophy is the supreme music" is purely Pythagorean; almost certainly it is a maxim of Pythagoras himself. It is to be understood by reference, first, to Pythagoras' teaching of "harmony," and, second, to his maxim that "music purges the soul, as medicine the body." It means that "philosophy," in the highest sense (and this sense is itself Pythagorean), is not the effort after mere knowledge, but an attunement of the human soul to the universal harmony; and that that is not true philosophy which does not produce this inward perfection. In other words, true science and true religion are veritably one.

This is, as Madame Blavatsky understood so well, a fundamental doctrine of Indian wisdom. Nor can any unbiassed student fail to be impressed by the astonishing resemblance of the Pythagorean teaching to the teaching of the purest Buddhism. Whether, as Madame Blavatsky believed, the resemblance is to be explained by actual contact between Pythagoras and Indian teachers, or whether, as Burnet held, it is due simply to the fact that meditation by profound natures upon the facts of human experience must ultimately lead to the same conclusions, I do not presume to decide. Nor does it seem to me an issue of great importance. What is important, and what it seems to me Madame Blavatsky was labouring heroically to impart to a materialised and sceptical world, is the truth that the fundamentals of the highest wisdom of Greece and of India were identical; and that in those fundamentals a positive and indisputable doctrine is contained—a genuine "theosophy." Pythagoras, whether by his own native and unaided genius, or by his contact with Eastern Sages, attained to this and taught it to his disciples. And from that teaching of Pythagoras immediately or mediately was derived all that two thousand five hundred years have proved to be most durable, most pregnant, and most precious in the religious wisdom of Greece. From Pythagoras it descended through

Plato to the neo-Pythagoreans and the neo-Platonists; from them it passed into the mysticism of the Christian Church, and as that Church grew rigid and formal, out of it again. It could blend naturally with the teaching of Jesus, just as the teaching of Jesus blends naturally with the teaching of Buddha; but *it could not blend with an external orthodoxy*. Always, as in the beginning, so in the end, it was a way of life, a Path, open to all men, essentially universal, wherein the faithful seekers of all nations meet and find themselves brothers indeed. No wonder then that Pythagoras who revealed this path to the Greek world was "exceedingly loved" for his gift to men.

P.S. I have foregone, in this brief sketch, even the most modest attempt to handle the Pythagorean doctrine of numbers. "Things *are* numbers," is his traditional assertion. There were later Pythagoreans who took that too literally, and assigned various numbers as the essential reality of various things and creatures. Burnet seems to me to stop half-way in his interpretation. He is right in insisting that the Pythagorean system of notation was different from any familiar to ourselves; and that the system (of which the "tetraktys" ⋰⋰ may serve as example) played an important part in the teaching of Pythagoras: but, in spite of his own recognition that the Pythagorean tradition must be sought in the writings of the later Pythagoreans, he makes no account of the obvious symbolic significance of such numerical arrangements. There is no doubt that the "tetraktys" and the pentagram served as secret signs in the early Pythagorean society. The "tetraktys" considered as a mere number, would not have been given such immense significance. It was also, I believe, a visible symbol of the gradual emanation of the world of existence from the Monad. In this more esoteric sense also, "things *were* numbers."

24

Pseudo-Mysticism and Modern Science

Before we can substantiate a charge of false mysticism, we need to have some clear conception of true mysticism.

Essentially, mysticism is the conviction of an all-pervading and all-embracing One. The Universe *is* a universe. It is obvious that to all modes of intellectual cognition this conviction can only be a hypothesis. The act of knowing involves a separation, and an opposition, of the knower and the known; therefore of an all-pervading and all-embracing Unity there can be no intellectual *knowledge*. Intellectual knowledge excludes unity; unity excludes intellectual knowledge.

Mysticism not merely admits, but insists upon this. Unity is not known, but given in immediate experience; and this immediate experience of unity is *known* to have been such only when the experience is at an end. An unique and ineffable experience totally different from any kind of intellectual cognition, and given under conditions which definitely exclude any kind of intellectual cognition, is averred to be the self-experience of the all-pervading One.

This experience stands perfectly secure from all intellectual criticism. Intellectual criticism may legitimately apply itself to the intellectual interpretations of this experience; but with the experience itself it can make no contact.

Aryan Path, January 1930.

It is clear that the conviction of an all-pervading Unity given in mystical experience is absolutely opposed to any form of religious or philosophical dualism. A real Unity cannot be half-hearted. Mind and matter, good and evil, may seem different enough in our practical lives, but the differences cannot be ultimate. They are differences necessarily established in the Unity by individual existences with the faculty of intellectual knowledge. Not that those who believe in the ultimate Unity of mysticism necessarily suppose that individual existence is a *defect*, though a nuance of this opinion is perceptible both in Platonism and Buddhism. It is just as consonant with the convictions of mysticism to believe that individual existence is a necessary means towards the self-explication and self-consciousness of the One. In order that the One shall be conscious of itself it needs the individual mind, and it needs the development of the mind to the point at which it recognises that its own inevitable intellectual perspectives are only perspectives. When a finite existence recognises the conditions of its own existence, and a finite mind recognises the conditions of its own operation, and these conditions are felt not as burdensome and oppressive, but merely as necessary, the pathway of the One into that individual existence is cleared of obstacles. The intellect has ceased to usurp a sovereignty to which it has no rightful claim.

Since Mysticism is irreconcilable with any Dualism, we have a short way of dealing with the assertions now frequently made by modern men of science that the modern scientific view of the world "leaves room for" Mysticism. Before being grateful for this condescension, we must inquire what kind of mysticism it is for which the modern scientist leaves room. If it is a dualistic mysticism, it is simply not mysticism; but an attempt to reimpose under that name the dualistic religion from which the Western mind is painfully struggling to free itself.

I cannot, in this brief space, permit myself the luxury of long quotations from such modern scientific apologists of 'mysticism' as Professors Eddington and Haldane. But it is true to say of both of them that the mysticism for which they wish to find room is a mysticism of 'values,' or of 'morality.' "The real world," as Professor Haldane puts it, "is the spiritual world of values." Without discussing whether this statement is true, or whether it has any *meaning*, we can state quite peremptorily that this 'mysticism' is not mysticism at all. Mysticism knows nothing of "a spiritual world of values" as distinct from a "material world of facts." The One of true mysticism is not the Good, or the True, or the Beautiful; it is the One. And in the One the Bad, the False, and the Ugly exist no less than the Good, the True, and the Beautiful. All alike, for true mysticism, are in some sense appearance. The goodness of the good thing is its element of appearance; because we call it good only in so far as, in some obvious or obscure manner, it promotes the fundamental propulsive energy of some individual human existences. And the badness of the bad thing is likewise its element of appearance. Their sheer existence alone is real.

True mysticism is beyond good and evil; and the mysticism which seeks to persuade itself or others that the One is good is a false mysticism. Mysticism does not seek to impose its personal terms upon the One. The One is not what we like, but that to which we and our likings belong. We cannot bargain with it, or propose conditions; and the true mystic has no desire to do so. That is what false mysticism finds it impossible to understand about true mysticism; for if it were possible for false mysticism to understand precisely that thing—that the true mystic has no desire that the One should be what he likes—false mysticism would become true.

Mysticism, by whatever path it is attained, demands the stripping off of our personalities from ourselves. We surrender them, it is true, only to receive them again. But the personality we receive again, is not the personality we surrendered. It is no longer we who like, or think, or do, but the One which likes, or thinks, or does in us.

And this impersonal personality we receive does not resemble the personal personality we surrendered. It is a new birth.

This impersonal personality can neither require, nor desire, that only the qualities it likes should qualify the One. The mere idea of such exclusiveness is strange, remote, fantastic. For the impersonal personality does not like things in the same way that the personal personality liked them. It is detached from them; it knows that its being does not depend on them; its affections towards them are disinterested. Therefore the desperate cry that what we love shall be eternal, and the desperate expedients by which some apparent answer to that cry is obtained, are alien to true mysticism.

In other words the validation of human ideals is no concern of true mysticism—with one great and momentous exception—the validation of the ideal of Unity itself. Mysticism claims that this ideal is real, and that it has direct experience of its reality. And precisely because this ideal *is* real, no other ideal can be real.

Now the 'mysticism' for which modern science, through the mouths of some of its chief expositors, seeks to make room is simply a 'mysticism' devoted to the validation of human ideals. Since human ideals are never complete (or they would not be ideals), the validation for human ideals is merely the perpetuation of Dualism. The good is real, the bad is not; spirit is real, matter is not; the 'ought' is real, the 'is' is not. The arguments by which these preferences are deified is childish. It runs thus: Since the exact sciences do not give us a picture of reality, something else must. It is not certain; but even if it were, there is no ground at all for assuming that the moral preferences of a civilized European scientist supply the picture of reality which we need.

Not that those preferences are vain. The choice is not between their nullity and their omnipotence. This kind of dilemma which haunts the soul of 'religion' and 'science' alike is simply ignored by mysticism. Man's preference for the good, like everything else, is for the mystic a

form taken by the One. It exists; and—this is the point—
the man in whom it truly and strongly exists does not
seek to have it validated. For him, and in him, it exists in
its own right. The good would not be more desirable if it
were proved to be the sole reality. "He who verily loves
God," said Spinoza, "cannot endeavour that God shall
love him in return." The demand that human ideals
shall be validated outside the human being, in whom
they are real as his own right hand, is simply the endeavour "that God shall love him in return."

True mysticism does not need to have room made for
it by science or any other mode of human knowledge. It
occupies no room which they can occupy, for it does not
exist in the same dimension. It is not an alternative, or a
possibility. It is the simple truth underlying all existence.
It is a certainty reached by the effort towards self-knowledge; it is simply the discovery that when the self is truly
known, there is no self to know or to be known,—but
only the One.

A selection of John Middleton Murry's critical essays which shows his involvement in the moral issues of the day, his interests, and his scholarship

In making this selection of John Middleton Murry's critical essays, Richard Rees has drawn heavily from the uncollected and unsigned articles written between 1919 and 1955. These articles, dating back to the years when the social trauma following two world wars weighted the human conscience, open to the reader Murry's deep sense of involvement in the moral issues of the day as well as the great range of his interests and his scholarship. So profound was his conviction of the need for the regeneration of society that this personal attitude permeated most of his critical writings.

Sir Richard has arranged the selections in three groupings—those dealing with poets, with critics, and with mystics. Whatever the work discussed in the first part—whether it treats Milton's Prosody, Shakespeare and Seneca, Hölderlin, or Proust, Joyce, Forster, and Lawrence—Murry discards the idea of art for art's sake and moves from a consideration of technique and style to that of "a living art" which may yield an "enrichment and refinement of experience." Hölderlin's significance to him is that he "sees all things in a cosmic or historical perspective." The world of Peacock, of Proust and Joyce, or Forster and Lawrence is the world of the present in which "spiritual greatness" must be tied to a "sense of mission." Lawrence's permanent rebellion against the state of society and his search for a new order approach the ultimate in this amplitude of mind.

The critics are seen in terms of their efforts to open larger worlds for their readers. In Trilling's *Matthew Arnold,* Murry enlarges on the idea of growth, of the initiation of men into the realm of "imaginative reason" and of living in the "grand style" according to a "hierarchy of values." The position taken in Empson's *Seven Types of Ambiguity* that verse gives pleasure because "one can reason about it" and the contention in the controversy between Tillyard and Lewis that reading makes possible contact "with the personality of the author" are alike rejected. Murry counters that reading militates to one end—sharing the "author's vision of things." Even on the matter of style, he quotes Flaubert, "c'est une manière de voir."

Freud's *Moses and Monotheism* and Eliot's *The Christian Society* lead the reader to Murry's thesis on mystics and the search for spirituality. The reemergence of Mosaic monotheism and the idea of a community of